Lean Procurement and Supply Chain Management: Key to Reducing Costs and Improving Profitability

By Ade Asefeso MCIPS MBA

Second Edition

ISBN-13: 978-1499755657

ISBN-10: 1499755651

Publisher: AA Global Sourcing Ltd
Website: http://www.aaglobalsourcing.com

Table of Contents

Disclaimer

This publication is designed to provide competent and reliable information regarding the subject matter covered. However, it is sold with the understanding that the author and publisher are not engaged in rendering professional advice. The authors and publishers specifically disclaim any liability that is incurred from the use or application of contents of this book.

Dedication

To my family and friends who seems to have been sent here to teach me something about who I am supposed to be. They have nurtured me, challenged me, and even opposed me…. But at every juncture has taught me!

This book is dedicated to my lovely boys, Thomas, Michael and Karl. Teaching them to manage their finance will give them the lives they deserve. They have taught me more about life, presence, and energy management than anything I have done in my life.

Chapter 1: Introduction

Procurement is the acquisition of goods or services. It is favourable that the goods/services are appropriate and that they are procured at the best possible cost to meet the needs of the purchaser in terms of quality and quantity, time, and location. Corporations and public bodies often define processes intended to promote fair and open competition for their business while minimizing exposure to fraud and collusion.

Almost all purchasing decisions include factors such as delivery and handling, marginal benefit, and price fluctuations. Procurement generally involves making buying decisions under conditions of scarcity. If good data is available, it is good practice to make use of economic analysis methods such as cost-benefit analysis or cost-utility analysis.

Global sourcing is a term used to describe practice of sourcing from the global market for goods and services across geopolitical boundaries. Global sourcing often aims to exploit global efficiencies in the delivery of a product or service. These efficiencies include low cost skilled labour, low cost raw material and other economic factors like tax breaks and low trade tariffs.

Common examples of globally sourced products or services include: labour-intensive manufactured products produced using low-cost Chinese labour, call centres staffed with low-cost English speaking workers in the Philippines and India, and IT work performed by low-cost programmers in India and Eastern Europe. While these examples are examples of Low-cost country sourcing, global sourcing is not limited to low-cost countries.

Majority of companies today strive to harness the potential of global sourcing in reducing cost. Hence it is commonly found that global sourcing initiatives and programs form an integral part of the strategic sourcing plan and procurement strategy of many multinational companies.

Global sourcing is often associated with a centralized procurement strategy for a multinational, wherein a central buying organization seeks economies of scale through corporate-wide standardization and benchmarking. A definition focused on this aspect of global sourcing is: "proactively integrating and coordinating common items and materials, processes, designs, technologies, and suppliers across worldwide purchasing, engineering, and operating locations.

The global sourcing of goods and services has advantages and disadvantages that can go beyond low cost. Some advantages of global sourcing, beyond low cost, include: learning how to do business in a potential market, tapping into skills or resources unavailable domestically, developing alternate supplier/vendor sources to stimulate competition, and increasing total supply capacity. Some key disadvantages of global sourcing can include: hidden costs associated with different cultures and time zones, exposure to financial and political risks in countries with (often) emerging economies, increased risk of the loss of intellectual property, and increased monitoring costs relative to domestic supply. For manufactured goods, some key disadvantages include long lead times, the risk of port shutdowns interrupting supply, and the difficulty of monitoring product quality.

Based on the consumption purposes of the acquired goods and services, procurement activities are often split into two distinct categories. The first category being direct, production-related procurement and the second being indirect, non-production-related procurement.

Direct procurement occurs in manufacturing settings only. It encompasses all items that are part of finished products, such as raw material, components and parts. Direct procurement, which is the focus in supply chain management, directly affects the production process of manufacturing firms. In contrast, indirect procurement activities concern "operating resources" that a company purchases to enable its operations. It comprises a wide variety of goods and services, from standardized low value items like office supplies and machine lubricants to complex and costly products and services; like heavy equipment and consulting services.

Chapter 2: History of Procurement

Prior to 1900, Procurement was recognized as an independent function by many railroad organizations, but in few other industries.

Prior to World War I, purchasing was regarded as primarily clerical.

During World War I & II – The function increased due to the importance of obtaining raw materials, supplies, and services needed to keep the factories and mines operating.

1950s and 1960s - Procurement continued to gain stature as the techniques for performing the function became more refined and as the number of trained professionals increased. The emphasis became more managerial; with introduction of major public bodies and intergovernmental organizations, such as United Nations, procurement become a well-recognized science.

1970s and 1980s - More emphasis was placed on Procurement strategy as the ability to obtain needed items from suppliers at realistic prices increased.

1983 - In September 1983, Harvard Business Review published a ground-breaking article by Peter Kraljic on purchasing strategy that is widely cited today as the beginning of the transformation of the function from

" Procurement," something that is viewed as highly tactical to procurement or supply management, something that is viewed as very strategic to the business.

1990s - Procurement starts to become more integrated into the overall corporate strategy and a broad-based transformation of the business function is ignited, fuelled strongly by the development of supply management software solutions which help automate the source-to-settle process.

2000s - The leader of the procurement function within many enterprises is established with a C-Level title - the Chief Procurement Officer (sometimes called the Head of Procurement). Websites, publications, and events, and that are dedicated solely to the advancement of Chief Procurement Officers and the procurement function arise. The global recession of 2008-2012 places procurement at the crux of business strategy.

2010s - The elevation of the function continues as Chief Procurement Officers are recognized as important business leaders and begin to take on broader operation responsibility.

Chapter 3: 5s Lean Procurement

Lean procurement should adapt the same concepts used in lean manufacturing. However these principles must be adapted to a service environment including key interfaces with suppliers. By working more closely with suppliers, the key element to lean purchasing is visibility into each other's operations. This should also include integrating resources to eliminate waste.

Some lean procurement processes are e-procurement and automated procurement. E-procurement conducts transactions, strategic sourcing, bidding, and reverse auctions using Web-based applications. Automated procurement uses software that removes the human element from multiple procurement functions and integrates with financials.

The key to lean procurement is visibility. Suppliers must be able to "see" into their customers' operations and customers must be able to "see" into their suppliers' operations. Organizations should map the current value stream, and together create a future value stream in the procurement process. They should create a flow of information while establishing a pull of information and products.

One of my colleagues at a group of company I use to work for concisely explains 5S for Manufacturing at one of our operations meeting and then conclude by asking the question. Is 5S Implementation Truly Worth the Effort? 5S, abbreviated from the Japanese words Seiri, Seiton, Seiso, Seiketsu, and Shitsuke, are simple but effective methods to organize the workplace.

I thought I'd try to answer the question in this book; how would a purchasing professional organize their buying categories? Here are my thoughts.

1. **Survey:** Gain a deep understanding of internal business needs, external market conditions and supplier capabilities for each buying category.
2. **Strategy:** develop a category sourcing strategy with a cross-functional team approach.
3. **Selection:** Based upon the strategy, select and contract with the supplier(s) that can meet the organization's needs based upon the sourcing strategy.
4. **Solutions:** Constantly challenge suppliers to drive continuous improvement to meet the quality, cost, service and innovation needs.
5. **Sustain:** Through relationship management measure, monitor and sustain supplier performance.

5S for purchasing doesn't exactly match 5S for manufacturing. For example, the visual tool aspect is missing. It should help manage the procurement process, deliver cost reduction and drive supplier continuous improvement.

Chapter 4: Lean Procurement

In the past decade the concept of Lean Manufacturing has picked up in a great deal. Companies are looking forward for reducing wastage in the system and improving performance and efficiency. This resulted in reduced inventory, increased throughput and improved customer service levels. Using the similar dynamic concept of lean companies is now moving fast ahead in Lean Procurement. This concept helps companies to broaden their framework of Lean concept deeper into their supply chain.

Lean Procurement is a long term commitment to combine elements of strategic sourcing and Lean principles. It provides visibility to suppliers about customers' current and future business and stressed at lasting, collaborative relationships with suppliers and business partners.

The key to lean Procurement is visibility. Suppliers must be able to "see" into their customers' operations and customers must be able to "see" into their suppliers' operations. Organizations should map the current value stream, and together create a future value stream in the procurement process. They should create a flow of information while establishing a pull of information and products. Lean purchasing calls for partnering with supplier and understand the total cost of doing business with a particular supplier.

The first step in conducting any type of Lean Sourcing initiative involves understanding where dollars/pounds are spent. Companies often track expenditures by supplier, but this approach is limiting, particularly if there are a large number of parts (e.g., over several thousand). Companies that manage their expenditures by part groupings or categories typically have a better handle on where their dollars/pounds go and can analyze pricing trends over time.

The Benefits of Lean Procurement

Lean Procurement provides four key benefits to organizations. These are:

1. Greater buy-in from key functional areas; operations and Procurement which care about both price and performance.
2. Greater likelihood of implementing identified sourcing savings.
3. Improved quality and reduced waste.
4. On-going additional cost reduction opportunities via collaboration with supply partners.

More advanced organizations that begin to experiment with lean Procurement quickly realize that strategic sourcing does not have to be in conflict with lean. Rather, they observe that strategic sourcing is really a precursor step to identifying long-term supply partners and more tightly coordinating purchasing efforts with operations and manufacturing.

They also realize that in an increasingly global supply market, conditions change and leading companies need to regularly go to the market to identify, qualify, benchmark, ensure best global supplier capability and competitiveness.

Today, Lean Procurement is making its way into the middle market, where smaller organizations are beginning to realize that strategic sourcing provides a means for substantial cost savings and at the same time addresses the concerns of operations personnel. Many are beginning to bridge the gap between procurement and operations by getting started with Lean Procurement. At its core, Lean Procurement is really about reducing Total Enterprise Cost.

Chapter 5: Lean Procurement is More than Ordering Materials

As someone who has expertise in both procurement and in lean, I have always been interested in what writers and pundits have to say about lean procurement. Mostly, they are saying that lean can help firms save on headcount in Procurement. But that is only part of the story of what lean procurement can do.

I was interested to read the April 1, 2012 article in Industry Week, Lean Procurement Processes Mean Fewer Employees by Becky Partida at APQC, which did a benchmarking study on the subject. The study focused on how many (full-time equivalent) FTEs was needed per $1B in purchases. The results are what one would expect: those organizations who were implementing lean in procurement needed fewer people. That metric is certainly telling and important. But it only tells part of the story in Procurement. The real story should be a lot more strategic.

There are so many other important and strategic factors that can impact the effectiveness and efficiency of Procurement. For example, adoption of supply management and supply chain technologies such as strategic sourcing software and spend analysis, when implemented properly, can help make procurement more lean. Organizations that perform supply base rationalization (and perform it well, of course) will be dealing with fewer, higher performing suppliers. Supplier proliferation is a major reason for increased transactions and waste in Procurement. Or take supplier performance management, which can't fall directly under the category of how many procurement folks does it take to manage purchases. It helps ensure a higher-performing supply base that requires less expediting results in higher quality and better responsiveness from suppliers and less cost and more value. This readily translates into a more efficient and cost-effective procurement operation.

Procurement can add to the top line as well as the bottom line as in collaborative product development with suppliers. When new products are being planned, involving suppliers in the process can be a value-added, cost-effective approach to consider. If an organization looks at lean procurement as only increased efficiency in pushing or eliminating paper and the processes surrounding that function, so many more value-added activities will be missed.

Just as lean manufacturing needs to be viewed more strategically than optimizing flow and pull in individual cells, lean procurement needs to be seen more strategically than just buyer transactions. It is so much more strategic than a process flow to buy "stuff". Looking at lean procurement only in terms of how many procurement (full-time equivalent) FTEs are buying products and services is to miss some of the biggest opportunities for making procurement lean and for adding value to the organization. It also reinforces the traditional and outdated view of Procurement as low-level paper pushers.

Lean Procurement delivers a defined process to:
1. Eliminate unnecessary activities.
2. Streamline supply chains.
3. Breakdown organisational 'silos'.
4. Reduce inconsistencies and eliminate duplication to avoid re-keying of data.
5. Re-use data down the supply chain to reduce costs improve discipline.
6. It provides data exchange standards.
7. Standardise documents and practices to streamline the procurement process for both the Buyer and the Vendor/Supplier/Contractor and in turn reducing the cost of procurement and reach out more to SMEs.
8. Reduced paperwork to create a paper free supply chain.
9. Allow orders to be placed and received faster.
10. Significantly reduce the time spent on the low value items.
11. Improve controls and accountability.
12. Aggregation of orders to deliver higher volume discounts where available.
13. Consolidation of invoices.
14. Data is always available online 24/7 for review.

Fundamentally lean process helps to reposition procurement; Lean Procurement eliminates waste, but don't neglect adding value.

What really is lean procurement?

From some of the descriptions of lean procurement that I have seen, it seems to have morphed into something that is either myopically focused and/or totally unrecognizable as lean to me.

Let's start with myopically focused. Yes, it is a good thing to do more with less, i.e., run procurement with fewer people. But what are the survivors doing? Are they focused primarily on transactions or are they focused on strategic activities? Reducing procurement headcount is much like reducing inventory in manufacturing. It is typically a by-product of lean, not a focus. It has to be done intelligently. Workflows need to become more efficient, and more importantly, the actual workflows and their underlying assumptions need to be questioned. When procurement asks; how would what I am doing add value to the customer (both internal and external), then many exciting possibilities will open up.

Lean procurement can be viewed as a way to:
1. Improve the procurement process and workflow, reducing time and eliminating waste.
2. Reduce/lower costs while improving the quality of products and services.
3. Improve the performance and responsiveness of suppliers.
4. Increase the focus on activities that add value to the firm.
5. Enhance procurement's strategic rather than transactional focus.

Many companies need to get beyond the notion that lean is primarily for manufacturing companies and the associates on the factory floor. While manufacturing historically has led the lean charge, opportunities can and should go well beyond it. It's natural to assume that lean means lean manufacturing, as it's the area that has gotten the most focus and has shown the most dramatic transformations. Lean procurement is applicable to all industries, in the manufacturing and service sectors.

Lean procurement questions why particular activities are being done and how to increase procurement's total value. Cost reduction is, of course, important. However, how lean helps procurement add value should remain foremost in mind. The lean mindset knows that adding value typically requires eliminating waste and cost. The approach to lean procurement should be holistic and not solely cost-focused.

Many tools in the lean toolset (value stream mapping, 5S, Kaizen, standard work) can apply. However, as in all lean practice, focus should be on the overall strategy, people and culture rather than primarily on the tools.

Chapter 6: Identifying Savings Opportunity in Your Procurement Path

The importance of purchasing in any firm is largely determined by four factors: availability of materials, absolute dollar/pound volume of purchases, percent of product cost represented by materials, and the types of materials purchased.

Most procurement departments have a good understanding of the most critical categories of goods and services that their organization buys; the direct materials, subcontracted services, and other things that are close to the core of what the organization is in business to do. Having such knowledge, illuminates the procurement departments regarding what they buy, how much they buy, who they buy from, and what fair market pricing is. This understanding enables these procurement departments to manage these critical categories well, achieving respectable cost savings and getting good supplier performance.

The Pareto's 20:80 rule however does not apply here since these critical categories only represent a small portion of the organization's overall spend (fraction of the line items purchased in a given year). Also, they only represent a minor percentage of the cost savings opportunities that the organization achieves in comparison to the actual potential.

Majority of the cost savings opportunities are hidden in the rest of the categories of goods and services that the organization buys. Because these categories have less visibility within the organization, they have been historically undermanaged, characterized by the use of too many suppliers and are bought at higher than benchmark prices.

Identifying these hidden opportunities is not very difficult. We will look at a 5 step process that helps organizations identify as well act upon the opportunities in these categories.

The 5 steps are:
1. Mine procurement information
2. Transform the procurement information
3. Identify sourcing opportunities
4. Execute sourcing opportunities identified
5. Calculate your savings

Step 1: Mine Procurement Information

Most organizations have some sort of electronic system in place for managing their purchase orders and supplier invoices. The data can be retrieved and used for identifying opportunities. Though the process sounds simple, the ground reality is that the quality of data mined from procurement and purchasing systems can at many times be difficult to comprehend. The poor quality can be in terms of nomenclature, material coding and at times even item description. Thus, availability of data will be of minimal use unless it is classified uniformly.

Step 2: Transform the Procurement Information

Once the data is mined, it's time to derive value by converting this raw, almost unusable data into actionable information that can be utilized to streamline your processes. There are several pieces of information you need from each record in the database; a clear description of what you've bought, a correct category, and the supplier. It often happens that a laptop is categorized under Office Supplies at one location and under mainframe purchases under another. Such disparities arise due to inaccurate categorization and different people involved in the data entry process. The same discrepancies can arise from entering vendor details resulting in one thinking of having more suppliers than what one actually has.

All of these very common errors can provide the procurement professional with data that is either less than adequate for a good sourcing initiative or, in the worst case, not usable at all. While the adage "garbage in, garbage out" held true and crippled many sourcing plans, there is a way to transform that "garbage" into more accurate information. That's called data cleansing. Adopting a uniform code can be a very good start to making your data actionable.

Step 3: Identify Opportunities

Once you have clean data, you are able to conduct a meaningful spend analysis. Simplified, spend analysis is the systematic review of historical purchase data. The output of spend analysis is a summary of purchases by various variables, such as category, supplier, and/or business unit.

The primary reason for conducting spends analysis is to identify opportunities for cost savings. The output for spend analysis is the identification of opportunities for cost savings.

Step 4: Execute on the Identified Opportunities

Once you have analyzed your spend and identified the categories to target for cost savings, the next step is to prioritize those opportunities and conduct sourcing initiatives for each.

The Easy Savings Categories: When launching a new process, starting with little risk and gradually accepting more is wise. So begin your strategic sourcing initiative with a category where success is easier to achieve. Simple categories like office supplies where several competent suppliers compete against each other with fervour may be the first place to look for easy savings.

Non-Traditional Categories: These areas include health benefits, advertising, travel, and fleet services. Identifying these areas and learning to work with your new internal customers is a challenge by itself. Some of these categories will require careful consideration and a very cautious, deliberate approach to supplier selection. But some of the categories will be a bit more straightforward. These more straightforward categories will enable you to use e-Sourcing, which has been a proven way of achieving higher degrees of cost savings compared to traditional competitive bidding. An e-Sourcing tool can provide benefits at each stage of the sourcing process;

1. Sourcing planning
2. Event creation
3. Supplier Evaluation and Award scenarios

An e-sourcing solution helps to reduce the time to source, reduces complexity in your sourcing process and increases the potential to generate savings from your current process. An e-sourcing application seamlessly integrated into a Spend Analysis solution can be a great enabler to realize maximum value from your Spend Data.

Step 5: Savings Calculations

Traditionally, cost savings is calculated by subtracting the new price from the baseline price and multiplying that difference by the current year's estimated quantity. Generally, that's a good starting point for estimating your cost savings. However, there are some potential adjustments you may want to make to your cost savings numbers.

Here are just a few:

1. Provide savings calculations which are accurate and actual rather than providing estimates and predictions.
2. Second, be careful in how you claim cost savings when quantities change from year-to-year. If your quantities are increasing by 50% from last year to this year while price goes down by 5% that means you are still buying

31

more than last year. Change in quantity should be compromised with the change in prices negotiated to report actual savings.

3. Calculate savings on a year-on-year basis comparing average prices from the previous year with that of the current year and state the quantum of savings.

Well, as you can see, it is possible for a procurement department to identify and act on cost savings opportunities, even when the starting point involves very bad data. While many people in the procurement field would consider overcoming the lack of data to be a gargantuan task, with five structured steps, you can deliver some real results. And the best part is none of this involves tediously long processes or resource investments. The primary enabler for all the steps here is the data that your organization will already possess. All that needs to be done is the establishment of the correct processes to ensure realization of these savings potential.

Chapter 7: Outsourcing of Specialized Business Processes

With the right approach, leadership, and support, outsourcing specialized services can exceed objectives and provide a competitive advantage for years.

Under constant pressure to slash costs, maximize throughput, and ensure premium quality, manufacturing companies are increasingly exploring outsourcing as a mechanism to drive rapid improvement and achieve best-in-class performance. This includes targeting core processes; ranging from specialized production (e.g., biopharmaceutical manufacturing, specifically engineered subcomponents) to differentiated customer support (e.g., white-glove service, 4-hour delivery window) to support highly customized systems and applications many of which have historically been dismissed as viable outsourcing candidates.

Outsourcing success is generally more achievable when limited to repeatable, transactional, low-complexity tasks, so some may assume that deciding to outsource judgment-based activities, critical processes, and even key differentiators ("specialized services") will certainly result in failure. However, this is not necessarily the case-while outsourcing specialized services presents additional challenges, with the right approach, leadership, and support, such outsourcing initiatives can exceed objectives and provide a competitive advantage for years.

Adopt a Collaborative Approach

Generally, when outsourcing commoditized activities (e.g., payroll, invoice processing), the scope of a prospective outsourcing relationship can be well-defined prior to engaging vendors, as proven capabilities to support these activities are commonly available from multiple outsourced vendors. The model for engaging with these vendors and the general approach for migrating to a vendor-provided solution is widely understood. Conversely, when outsourcing specialized services, organizations are attempting to find or create a market capability that may not exist in a mature form. This creates a challenge, even for organizations with prior outsourcing experience (and success), as it requires an alternative approach to engaging potential vendors; most likely involving a jointly developed solution with a trusted vendor partner, rather than relying on a vendor to provide an "off the shelf" solution.

In some respects, this collaborative approach resembles the means adopted two decades ago, when companies first began to seriously consider contracting with third parties to provide critical business processes and services. Vendors worked collaboratively with clients to accommodate unique business needs, often through developing processes, tools, systems, and applications that later evolved into 'solution enablers' to drive efficiency and productivity. This joint venture approach, where the vendor and the client work synergistically to develop a new but efficient capability, is essential when outsourcing specialized services.

Address Scope with Modular Design

One of the first challenges companies face with specialized services outsourcing is defining scope as a ready-made option that encompasses all elements of the desired solution. There are often grey areas around discretionary elements of scope, depending on the cost, service levels, and terms, which are often complementary to the core solution, but are not aligned with proven and mature capabilities demonstrated by vendors in the marketplace (in some cases vendors may not even have an interest in providing such services). As an example, a contract manufacturer may lack expertise in providing operational support functions, such as finance and accounting or tax reporting expertise, or may not have the technical capability to build and maintain an operational data store. As a result, when outsourcing a specialized process, portions of the resultant Request for Proposal (RFP) may more closely resemble a Request for Information (RFI), as companies attempt to understand vendor offerings and capabilities via open-ended requests for approach descriptions, rather than precise, close-ended requirements.

While this approach is somewhat contrary to the typical competitive sourcing approach, the ability to evaluate both proposed solution descriptions and compliance with known requirements will allow companies to more precisely focus outsourcing efforts on scope elements for which vendors have offered a compelling solution. Therefore, a modular approach to outsourced services, where particularly troublesome or non-competitive elements of scope can be isolated and excluded from the final services solution, allows companies to execute a contract that strikes the right balance between proven vendor capabilities and willingness to develop a solution that meets all quality, accuracy, and cost requirements.

Set Expectations around Benefits Realization

As establishing and managing expectations appropriately is also integral to the success of specialized services outsourcing, initiative sponsors must set and communicate realistic expectations about implementation timing and the realization of benefits. Complex one-of-a-kind services often require more time to yield the quality improvements, efficiency enhancements, and cost savings than do more traditional outsourced services, due to the time required to develop customized solutions, document processes, train resources and stabilize an outsourced environment.

Consequently, the return on investment for outsourcing specialized services is typically measured in years rather than months, and the contract term will likely need to be longer to offset the increased risks and investment required by the vendor. This is especially true if the vendor is limited in leveraging any developed tools, processes, and systems for other clients due to the unique nature of the services. In this case, the vendor is likely sharing in the risk and investment, which will be reflected in the cost of the services.

Be Flexible with Vendors

Possibly the most important element in successfully outsourcing specialized services is ensuring that the corporate decision-making body is committed to being flexible. Even if vendors have proven experience and capability to perform some of the requested scope, they may need to partner with other providers (with whom they may or may not have existing relationships), or may need to develop the processes, systems and capable resources to perform the full scope of services. Additionally, mandating that vendors develop solutions that are "unnatural" for them increases the likelihood that they will drop out of the competitive process or provide solutions so riddled with assumptions and caveats that they barely resemble the final, contracted solution. Therefore, companies need to be nimble enough to course-correct throughout the sourcing and solution development processes, as opposed to dogmatically adhering to a sourcing strategy that may become increasingly implausible.

Outsourcing even the most mature, transactional, and simple activities is challenging given the change management implications, supplier relationship management requirements, and requisite level of organizational and process maturity. While incorporating the above-listed attributes into an outsourcing approach does not guarantee success of a specialized services outsourcing initiative, companies can realize a much higher rate of success if they employ a well-conceived strategy, leverage a modular sourcing approach, set appropriate expectations for the realization of benefits, and ensure the flexibility to adjust in response to inevitable obstacles as they are faced. With these foundational elements in place, companies will be well positioned to reap the benefits and competitive advantages of specialized services outsourcing.

Imperative to the success of any outsourcing arrangement is selecting the right partner with which to do business. One selection tactic is simply to choose the lowest-cost vendor and if all other factors are equal, that may be the best route to go. However, the "other factors" frequently are essential considerations.

When selecting a strategic partner, look for one who has a vision around improving productivity, transforming processes, as well as providing cost savings and work closely with the internal team to develop reasonable short-term objectives and also the long-term ideal environment; continuously invest in their technology and services delivery platform; utilize proven management tools and continuous improvement programs, such as Lean Six Sigma; and provide a strong change management and training program for employees.

Chapter 8: Skills for the Lean Supply Chain and Purchasing Professional

There are really two ways to think about a supply chain. One is a market of many bidders orchestrated by Purchasing. The second is a stable set of partnerships with a small number of suppliers created by Purchasing. In the fading world of mass production the overwhelming choice of supply chain professionals was to orchestrate markets: Set qualifying standards and encourage as many bidders as possible. Then depend on market dynamics to drive suppliers to higher levels of efficiency while providing lower prices and better service to the buyer.

In the emerging world of lean production, supply chain managers seek to create win-win relationships with a small and stable supply base by focusing on the shared value creation process; what we call the value stream that flows through the supplier firm into the buyer firm.

Instead of accepting the pricing, quality, delivery, and flexibility levels offered by the best current supplier, the lean supply chain manager works with suppliers to challenge every step in the value creating process and gradually move it toward perfection.

Doing this involves an entirely different set of skills from traditional mass-production purchasing. In particular, it requires that purchasing managers learn to see the value stream; the sequence of value creating steps required to design, make, and deliver the product and learn to remove the waste, mistakes, and rigidities. Instead of awaiting successful results as the market grinds on the suppliers, lean purchasing professionals focus relentlessly on improving the value creating process to insure successful outcomes.

Purchasing managers can draw a simple value-stream map for a given component stretching all the way from raw materials into the hands of the end customer. The map shows every step involved in the 'current state' of the value stream, including the value of each step, and the time and effort required. From the current-state map it's easy to apply lean principles to create a 'future state' and even an 'ideal state' that the supplier should be able to achieve by working with the purchaser.

Purchasing Managers and buyers should walk through their value streams to be able to understand the tools purchasing staff need to move from mass to lean.

One of the most striking aspects of these walks is the initial assumption of purchasing managers that what goes on inside their own organization is irrelevant to supplier performance. Their attitude almost invariably is that suppliers are there to do everything they can to make the customer happy and to be replaced if they can't. Then, as they walk along the value stream, the reality gradually begins to dawn that supplier costs are in many cases the direct consequences of customer behaviour; Out-of-control engineering change processes that require repeated adjustments to production activities at the supplier; sclerotic process certification requirements which discourage suppliers from performing kaizen on their processes; and erratic schedules from customers that bear no relation to daily shipping requirements. One of the key findings always is that purchasing must look inward at the rest of its own firm as well as outward at the supply base.

The awareness building on these walks goes the other way as well. As they proceed, suppliers routinely state that they have already done 'the lean thing' and have examples of 5S, set-up reduction, cellular manufacturing, and poka-yokes for quality improvements to demonstrate this. The sad fact I often observe is that the purchasing professionals have absolutely no capacity to evaluate these claims; many of which are bogus. Nor do they have the skills to point out the root causes of waste in supplier operations. From their past experience, the buyers know how to take bids and how to play suppliers against each other, but they usually have no knowledge of how to raise the performance of even the best suppliers to a higher level while removing fundamental causes of cost.

This then is the new challenge for lean purchasing. Every Senior Manager and every buyer need to gain the fundamental knowledge required to analyze every value stream and create a plan for essential improvements. This takes time and effort and results are only achieved slowly at the start. But the improvements are continuous and accelerate over time. By contrast, the market-based approach, in which the buyer never examines its own behaviour and simply looks for new supply sources to keep the pressure on existing suppliers, can produce quick results. And the recent experiments with reverse auctions produced initial results even faster. But then performance plateaus or even falls backwards as suppliers conclude they can no longer work for tiny or even negative margins. What else can be expected when no attention has been paid to fundamental cost drivers? And there is little prospect of further improvement.

Where do you stand as a supply professional? Here's a simple test:

1. If you are currently calling your suppliers to talk about price and to demand price reductions without specific reference to cost drivers, you are a mass production supply chain manager.

2. If you are calling to talk about the value creation process and specifically how to reduce costs (and prices) by taking out wasted steps along every value stream while improving quality and responsiveness, you are a lean supply chain manager.

I hope you are becoming the latter. I am certain that the future lies with the lean supply chain and the lean purchasing organization, as pioneered many years ago by Toyota.

Chapter 9: Procurement should be Strategic and Lean

In those good old days, companies proudly maintained giant inventories of "safety stock," had dramatic levels of work-in-process, piled unusable items out of sight for possible later scrutiny, and threw hoards of people at any problem. Very little mattered except being able to keep churning out sellable products for product-hungry consumers. Profits were high and the world seemed very good!

Today's most successful businesses; whether small, medium or big, know the concepts and benefits of rock-bottom 3rd decimal point pricing, global sourcing, integrated supply chains, on-site supplier services, phased deliveries, risk-sharing, and consistently acceptable quality. This is the domain of Strategic Procurement.

Lean Six Sigma Reference for Procurement Professionals

A list of lean Six Sigma definitions that should come in handy.

Six Sigma: A means of progressively improving operational performance through process and design optimization. The term specifically refers to a quality standard equivalent to 3.4 defects per million opportunities.

Master black belts: Black belts who consistently deliver high performance. They lead complex projects and deliver internal training and mentoring.

Black belts: Team members who have implemented at least one project and have demonstrated mastery of Six Sigma methods and tools.

Green belts: Team members trained in basic Six Sigma techniques who support black belt projects or run their own.

Yellow belts: Team members with basic Six Sigma training.

DMAIC: Abbreviation for a framework for improving processes. The steps are define, measure, analyze, improve and control.

DMEDI: Abbreviation for a framework for creating and optimizing new processes. The steps are define, measure, explore, develop and implement.

Jidoka: A quality control process that involves stopping the manufacturing line when a defect or abnormality is detected.

Kaizen: Japanese for continuous improvement.

Kan-ban: Used in a "pull" system of manufacturing precisely driven by demand, as opposed to the traditional "push" manufacturing philosophy, in which inventories can pile up. A Kan-ban is a bin or container that can hold only the amount needed by the customer.

Chapter 10: Lean Sourcing Creates Sustainable Purchasing Savings

In the past decade the concepts of "lean" and "strategic sourcing" both made it onto the corporate main stage, separately capturing the executive and media spotlight. Outsiders viewed lean as an art practiced by operational wizards or "Six Sigma Black Belts," adept at reducing waste and improving performance and efficiency. Lean achieved its magic by introducing new production and operational processes that improved organizational productivity. In the case of manufacturing, this resulted in reduced inventory, increased throughput and improved customer service levels.

Lean also stressed lasting, collaborative relationships with suppliers and business partners. Above all, as its supporters preached, lean is a journey, implemented through continuous Kaizen improvements. A lean transformation could take several years and typically involves complete process re-engineering. But lean success stories slowly began to emerge that captured the imagination of executives, making the time spent well worth it. Toyota's lean success illustrated to executives worldwide that lean could transform production and quality standards for an entire industry, changing the basis of competition.

Across the manufacturing sector, many organizations began to understand the improvements that lean could achieve. But the art of lean was still very much a mystery to many on the outside.

In contrast, strategic sourcing stormed onto the stage in a take no prisoners, hammer-driven approach to cost reduction that was easy to understand. Strategic sourcing was everything lean was not; a one-time effort, a quick hit without any major internal process changes that was less than fully data driven. If lean was the Eastern medicine that focused on treating the corporate patient holistically over time; requiring active involvement on the patient's behalf in improving his condition strategic sourcing was the prescription drug that immediately got its adherents hooked on quick-fix savings. Popping the Sourcing Pill.

How did strategic sourcing generate results? It treated the corporate patient by introducing a new type of structured tender and bidding process into purchasing (with increased competition and greater price transparency). As with cholesterol reducing drugs, patients saw the impact of strategic sourcing almost immediately (but in a similar vein, the underlying cause of the maladies often went unaddressed).

Strategic sourcing was able to achieve tremendous savings for many of its adopters because 70% of a company's purchasing costs, on average, are tied up in what is being bought (the balance of the costs cover inventory, inventory carrying costs, procurement personnel and 'maverick buying'). However, most companies historically had tended to focus on inventory reduction (which Lean and other initiatives addressed). When companies began to tackle purchasing cost reduction through strategic sourcing, the results could impact operating performance in months, not years (and without the serious collaboration of different internal teams). Dozens of research studies confirmed this as well. £1 saved through sourcing efforts was worth an estimated £5–£25 in increased sales.

According to experts who lauded its adoption, the miracle of strategic sourcing was here to stay. But many purchasing organizations that implemented strategic sourcing processes and technology began to realize that they were leaving additional savings on the table and perhaps most important, were not creating long-term sustainable partnerships with their supply base to improve other elements of supplier performance beyond price (e.g. on-time deliveries and quality). To go after these additional opportunities, some of these purchasing organizations began to coordinate their efforts with supply chain and operational executives inside their organizations. Thus, Lean Sourcing was born.

Chapter 11: Getting Started with Lean Sourcing

Lean Sourcing provides four key benefits to organizations. These are:

1. Greater buy-in from key functional areas; operations and purchasing which care about both price and performance.
2. Greater likelihood of implementing identified sourcing savings.
3. Improved quality and reduced waste.
4. On-going additional cost reduction opportunities via collaboration with supply partners.

More advanced organizations that begin to experiment with lean sourcing quickly realize that strategic sourcing does not have to be in conflict with lean. Rather, they observe that strategic sourcing is really a precursor step to identifying long-term supply partners and more tightly coordinating purchasing efforts with operations and manufacturing. They also realize that in an increasingly global supply market, conditions change and leading companies need to regularly go to the market to identify, qualify, benchmark, ensure best global supplier capability and competitiveness.

Today, Lean Sourcing is making its way into the middle market, where smaller organizations are beginning to realize that strategic sourcing provides a means for substantial cost savings and at the same time addresses the concerns of operations personnel. Many are beginning to bridge the gap between procurement and operations by getting started with Lean Sourcing.

Companies that manage their expenditures by part groupings or categories typically have a better handle on where their dollars/pounds go and can analyze pricing trends over time.

Aggregating purchasing volume and dollars/pounds using a Pareto Analysis (or the 80/20 rule by examining the 20% of purchases that comprise 80% of the total costs) begins to show where the largest cost savings opportunities might lie and which initiatives would have the biggest impact on the company. In addition, our experience suggests that companies that regularly cast their nets "wide" to identify alternative suppliers achieve the most significant cost savings.

Furthermore, from a "live-bidding event" standpoint, companies that identify six or more market participants typically generate greater savings than companies who include fewer suppliers.

Performance and Partnering

Performance measurement is often an indicator of the level of purchasing process capability within an organization. These specific metrics begin to help organizations understand the total cost of doing business with a particular supplier. Companies that have developed a means to look beyond piece part pricing often squeeze out additional cost-savings opportunities. Increased defects at a lower purchase price can often increase total cost of ownership.

Companies that implement and have formal processes in place to develop suppliers typically receive the benefits of cost reduction on an on-going basis. Companies that don't measure their suppliers typically have a challenging time quantifying the cost of quality. More advanced companies who have deployed lean sourcing initiatives often work collaboratively with their supply partners on an ongoing basis. For example, a prominent Tier 1 automotive company deployed a supply management team to help streamline and squeeze out inefficiencies at their Tier 2 partner.

(In the automotive industry, the perception is that when a supply management team is deployed it must mean the supplier is near bankruptcy not an entirely accurate perception) When deployed proactively, the Tier 2 supplier becomes not only more cost effective for that Tier 1 but more competitive in general and better able to compete for new business.

In addition, joint product innovation can provide new growth opportunities for key suppliers. Even in rather standard hard core industrial products, a little product innovation goes a long way.

Developing a stamped product to do what formerly was a casting has real savings potential. New engineered products combining hybrid plastic injection moulded parts with metal parts can improve performance, reduce weight, reduce welds, reduce shop floor area and integrate functions. The savings are often enormous often in the area of 50–75%.

Lean Sourcing requires a long-term commitment to combining elements of strategic sourcing with lean principles. It is not a destination, but a journey, that has different stages of maturity along the way.

Packing for the Trip

Lean Sourcing success requires that organizations; create a Lean Sourcing process that can be mapped and communicated to all team members Open communication and participation across functional areas provides a couple of significant benefits. First, open communication facilitates fairness and buy-in across the company. Second, greater cross-functional input provides a more comprehensive view of the issues that impact the company. By incorporating multiple views, solutions can be developed which address problem areas.

1. Develop project milestones, deadlines and target dates to get the job done. This is self-explanatory but accountability drives results. A never ending start or end date results in malaise and weak execution.

2. Create a team member incentive structure and compensation plan tied to process outcomes. We have seen incentive structures that are actually incompatible with such a process (e.g. a plant manager earns a bonus based on company sales instead of quality or total landed cost). Develop bonus structures and

cash compensation that are awarded back to employees that identify and help implement cost reduction initiatives.

Chapter 12: Lean Purchasing and What it Can Mean to you and Your Company

As a national average, 60% of the cost to manufacture is attributable to purchased materials. If the purchasing function controls over 60% of the costs in a product, then resources and talent must be focused on this function if the business is to stay healthy.

What should be emphasized is the establishment of business relationships and arrangements with suppliers as a primary task and satisfaction as a primary measurement. Emphasis on placing purchase orders and on expediting delivery should be minimized. Can today's suppliers grow with us and supply the technologies and capacity required for our future needs? What strategic alliances with suppliers will be required in the future? What roles will price and quality play in the product sourcing decisions of the future?

Purchasing establishes and maintains the supplier base, seeing to it that adequate capacity and quality are available and that the level of service and price are optimal. To accomplish that requires purchasing to develop your suppliers. You need suppliers who are dependent upon your company's success and are willing to work closely with you.

Lean and Inventory Management

The only good reason for maintaining inventory is that conditions exist that makes it less costly to have it than not to have it. If a supplier doesn't deliver on time, extra inventory compensates for the problem and allows operations to continue. It also makes us an enabler and sends a wrong signal to the supplier. Inventory is a RESULT and very expensive. Inventory simply hides problems. Drain the inventory and expose the problems. Now you can deal with them.

Problems covered by inventory:
1. Unpredictable customer demand.
2. Inaccurate forecasts.
3. Low process yields, scrap, rework.
4. Incoming materials rejects.
5. Unreliable supplier deliveries.
6. Equipment availability.
7. Missed production schedules.
8. Field failures, customer returns.

Fact: The longer the lead-time the greater the need for more inventory and the greater the costs.

Fact: The longer inventory sits, the harder it is to move.

Fact: The cost of carrying inventory has been looked upon by accounting as strictly a dollar item based upon what you paid for it. The TRUTH is, you are looking at roughly 75%/year of the purchase price, or 1.5% per week.

We keep trying to solve problems with increased inventory. And price increases are only an enabler for the habit. The only way to reduce inventory is reduce the lead-time. The only way to reduce the lead-time is to reduce your process cycle time. The way to do that is to reduce your set up time.

The Problem with Inventory

1. When the market or technology changes, all you have is worthless inventory.
2. It is expensive to hold on to.
3. It requires support resources of people, systems, equipment and transactions.
4. It is difficult to work around.
5. Eventually it becomes not worth what you paid for it.
6. It can be a coping mechanism that hides the real problems.

We need to move from Supplier Managed Inventories to Supplier Managed Deliveries.

1. Identify the demand.
2. Produce and deliver to that demand.
3. Deliver to point of use.
4. Monitor and adjust to usage.

Chapter 13: Elements of Lean Purchasing and Good Supplier

Look at the products you purchase not by price but by priority.

You have A, B, and C items. An A item is one that is extremely critical and will shut you down. Price does not matter. It's the criticality of the item.

Sell what your are producing at the time you produce it. Get rid of inventory by eliminating lead times.

If it cost 1.5% per week to hold something, the very same number applies to the manufacturer, the distributor and the customer.

It all comes down to the supplier's lead time versus when you need it, versus the price of inventory.

The point is that the item may appear to be less expensive than the competition, but their lead time can really cost you.

In working with a supplier, why not have them ship to you out of inventory for the first 4 months. Afterward, they have to ship directly off their manufacturing line.

Elements of Lean Purchasing
1. Collapsed cycle times.
2. Speed replaces inventories.

3. Direct links to top suppliers.
4. Appropriate quality for the particular application is a given.
5. Direct user/provider interface.
6. The deeper the supply chain, the better.

Elements of a Good Supplier
1. Has minimized cycle times.
2. Quality is appropriate. (Process capability).
3. Owns logistics transport and Point of use deliveries.
4. Assists in the design of components and products.
5. Knows your business/customers.
6. Knows why they are profitable.
7. Is a technology leader in their field?
8. Prices based on a superior process.
9. Personnel turnover <5% per year.

Example:
Let's say you have a product that takes 12 minutes to produce, but it has an 8-week lead time. To determine the Velocity ratio you would do the following:

60 (minutes) x 8 (hours) x 5 (days) x 8 (weeks) = 19,200 minutes ÷ 12 minutes = 1:1600

The question becomes, if it takes 12 minutes to produce a part, why is there an 8 week lead time?

Our suppliers have to get their Process Cycle Time reduced. To do that means reducing WIP while increasing output. Furthermore, by making everything happen faster, you also improve cash flow. Because the faster it all happens, the faster you get paid.

The time has come for us to be thinking in terms of Contribution to Profit instead of Controlling Costs.

If Purchasing Wants to Become Lean
1. Buy from lean suppliers.
2. Key suppliers must have lead times no greater than your needs.
3. Each week of lead time costs you 1.5% per week of the price.
4. Suppliers cannot hide behind inventory.
5. Suppliers' quality system must match your product needs.
6. Purchasing must buy affordable cost.
7. Contribution to profit not PPV (Purchase Price Variance), cost reduction.

Invite the owners of your top 20 suppliers, or the highest official person you can, to your company for lunch (I use to call this suppliers summit). Explain to them what your company is all about and where your company is going. Explain to them what we need from them to help us get from where we are now to where it is we need to be. Educate them on Lean if they aren't already. Ask them to declare who wants to come with us right then, there and now.

Explain to them that you are seeking a business partner. That you want a business strategy not an individual package with each supplier. Then hold a one day seminar at the suppliers' site talking to their employees about lean.

A key role of purchasing is to build roads of communication between your company and your suppliers. In doing so, you must:
1. Define Quality. What is it?
2. Listen to suppliers' issues.
3. Resolve historic issues – engineering, personnel, broken promises, singed fingers, etc.
4. Establish lines of communications, people and systems.
5. Agree on quality definitions.

Chapter 14: Is ERP Enabler or Business Streamliner?

Today, most business processes are enabled through technology. That should ideally put technologists in an enviable position. But the reality is far from it, technology actually gets a pretty bad rap when it comes to such assessment from the business. Most often, from the business's point of view, technology fails to create significant value, fails to deliver the promised efficiencies and the desired value on the investments. This is true for most major corporate IT initiative, whether they were a result of business driving technology or the other way around. Most supply chain initiatives have a large functional and organization footprint and therefore, often fall into a similar trap. But is technology really to blame for the low returns or is there more to it?

When firms invest in packaged business solutions, one of the most common and a misguided expectation is that the solution will fully enable their existing processes. This is misguided because the packaged software solutions are built to provide only a certain amount of process support that is (1) common across industries and (2) generally considered the best practice in an industry/segment. None of which ensures that the solution will fully enable their existing processes. To make matters worse, such business initiatives generally do not involve any planned changes in the business process even when the existing processes do not fully support the needs. In fact, most of the initiatives do not involve any capability assessment to ensure that the business processes are designed to support the business strategy and the advantages it seeks to create.

No wonder, a large number of such ill-planned initiatives fail to produce the expected results. 30% to 50% of ERP projects are thought to be "failures" by the people who were thinking of implementing one. But this may just be another "urban myth", because of the unrealistic expectations of the organization from a technology. I think that an ERP should be seen more like an "infrastructure" (enabling transaction processing, data management, process integration and information access) rather than the "streamlined (business) processes". ERP should be viewed as the stable infrastructure that allows an organization to create and deploy the kind of innovation and differentiation that drives real business improvements.

That is my view; technology is simply an enabler. The differentiation and hence the competitive advantages can be created only through business capabilities that are superior to others. Such superiority is never an accident, but must be a result of deliberate design of business processes that support your strategy.

Chapter 15: Offshore Sourcing

Offshore sourcing in itself is not a new phenomenon. It is estimated that more than 75% of American and British corporations are engaged in international sourcing. However, the changes in the last couple of years warrant that the decisions for offshore sourcing be re-evaluated. The changes in cost of fuel, regulatory environment, and the recession are several reasons driving such evaluation. To evaluate the offshore sourcing decisions made in the last few years, it is imperative to understand the drivers, considerations, and the effects of offshore sourcing on the supply chain.

The most overwhelming reason for the companies to offshore source is the lure of reducing the cost of merchandise. A recent study on offshore or near shore; found that lower costs were the driving factor in the offshore sourcing decisions for 79% of the respondents in the survey. That is an overwhelming number, but it is not surprising. What is surprising is how little the companies usually know about the total cost of their offshore sourced products. Most companies do not have any established process or system to collect and compute the total landed costs for their products. While the cost of merchandise is easily obtained from the purchase orders, the other costs like transportation and warehousing are harder to establish and accurately allocate to products.

Most companies have questionable processes to capture and allocate these costs. The value of ordered products is the most commonly used factor for allocation of logistics (transportation and warehousing) costs. However, these costs should be better allocated using the handling and storage characteristics of the products rather than simply using their value. A set of outdoor garden furniture is always going to have a substantially higher cost of transportation, handling, and stocking in the warehouse than a Computer game system, even though they may both have comparable purchase costs. The solution lies in capturing transportation costs using the weight and volume characteristics, warehouse handling costs using activity based costing, and warehouse stocking costs using the number of days and space utilized by a product stocked in the warehouse.

But, these three components only make part of the total cost of the products, other costs such as the cost of receiving, unpacking, and making it ready for the sales floor and the cost of promotion and clearance. These costs become significant for the offshore sourced products simply because of the longer replenishment lead-time, which means that the demand forecasts driving the replenishments must be made for longer time horizons which tend to be less accurate than the short-term demand forecasts. Less accurate demand forecasts mean higher promotion and clearance budgets and in some cases, additional logistics costs associated with warehousing and dynamic inventory re-balancing to move products within the network where they can potentially fetch better prices. All of these factors add costs that are complex to model and capture, and harder to correctly allocate for any meaningful comparison among products.

Considerations for Sourcing Decisions

Given the firm has a clear understanding of the total costs, what other factors should be considered for making sourcing decisions? Here are some considerations that would directly affect your total costs and should be considered for any offshore sourcing decision. Not only do they affect the direct costs, but they also add process complexity that the corporation must be ready to deal with.

1. **Regulations and Trade Agreements:** What are the regulatory requirements for the products under consideration? Most of the international trade is subject to additional taxes, excise duties; value added taxes (VAT), etc. Find out how this adds up to the total cost of the products when offshore sourced. Find out if there are any trade agreements favourable to the products under consideration. These agreements may reduce your duties and taxes, or provide other financial incentives. The international trade is also subject to regulatory process a requirement which means the importer typically has more paper work to prepare and file with the customs. Managing the extra paperwork is bound to add to your costs as this requires more processes, systems, or a contract with a service provider.

2. **Type of Merchandise:** Not all merchandise is equally suitable for offshore sourcing. Products that are innovative, fashion, and highly seasonal in nature may not be suitable for offshore sourcing due to volatile nature of demand. These types of products require the ability to quickly react to the demand by either increasing the supplies or shutting them down, both of which are easier with shorter replenishment times. Other products that are more utilitarian in nature and have relatively stable demand may be good candidates for offshore sourcing.

3. **Financing and Payment Terms:** offshore sourcing may involve financial terms that are typically different from those in domestic sourcing situations. Make sure that the added complexity of procedures, advance financing, and/or guarantees are considered in making the case for offshore sourcing.

4. **Multi-modal Transportation and Port Management:** Managing the product at the port, loading, unloading, customs-clearance, and onwards shipment adds to the costs as well. Managing multi-modal transportation needs more complex systems for planning, optimization, and execution of the shipments. While this can be outsourced to a logistics provider, corporations may lose the opportunity to optimize their transportation spend.

Finally, ensure that you have the systems in place to provide inventory visibility for the products in transit, which may allow you to dynamically plan their final destination as the ship moves closer to the home port to better match with any changes in demand during the time in-transit.

Offshore sourcing: Effect on Supply Chain

All sourcing decisions affect the supply chains in several ways. They affect the costs as well as the ability of the supply chain to respond to changes in demand and supply. Evaluating how the supply chain will react to off-sourcing and ensuring that it is designed to address the process requirements involved in the offshore sourcing is paramount for a successful execution of such decisions.

1. **Costs:** Offshore sourcing almost always will have additional supply chain costs in freight, inspection, financial instruments, drayage management, trade tariffs, and costs related to managing these processes. Make sure that these have been thought and properly estimated for an objective decision making exercise.

2. **Lead-time:** Offshore sourcing also typically results in much longer replenishment lead-time to the plants, warehouses, and stores. The effect of a longer lead-time on the supply chain is the reduced ability to react to changes in demand and supplies. This causes considerable strain on the processes, calls for

more accurate demand forecasts, relatively stable demand, and reliable supplies.

3. **Risk:** Increased costs, replenishment lead-time, and length of the supply chain all add to the supply chain risk. Longer chain and additional nodes provide new points of failure in the supply chain and substantially increase the risk of disruption, making it prone to factors that are not typical in domestic supply chains such as international politics, wars, and piracy.

Many companies are considering or re-evaluating offshore sourcing due to changes in the business environments such as cost of fuel, regulatory environment, and the ongoing sluggishness in the economy. Successful re-evaluation requires that the managers clearly understand the drivers, considerations, and the effects of offshore sourcing on the supply chain. Only an objective analysis of all these aspects can help establish the true value of off-sourcing for a company.

Chapter 16: What is Lean Supply Chain Management

Lean is how a properly designed and operated supply chain should function. A lean supply chain process has been streamlined to reduce and eliminate waste or non-value added activities to the total supply chain flow and to the products moving within the supply chain. Waste can be measured in time, inventory and unnecessary costs. Value added activities are those that contribute to efficiently placing the final product at the customer. The supply chain and the inventory contained in the chain should flow. Any activity that stops the flow should create value. Any activity that touches inventory should create value.

What must be done to be lean?

Supply chains gain waste and non-value added activities for many reasons, both internal to the company and external. Regaining the lean supply chain may mean addressing many of the same issues that created the problems of extra and unneeded time, inventory and costs.

The ideal approach is to design the perfect supply chain and fit your company's operation onto it. Supply chain management is meant to reduce excess inventory in the supply chain. A supply chain should be demand driven. It is built on the pull approach of customers pulling inventory, not with suppliers pushing inventory. Excess inventory reflects the additional time with the supply chain operation. So the perfect supply chain would be lean with removing wasteful time and inventory.

A supply chain, with the pull, flows back from deliveries to the store or to the customer warehouse back through to purchase orders placed on suppliers. Anything that delays or impedes this flow must be analyzed as a potential non-value added activity.

To develop a lean supply chain, firms should

1. Understand lean is an ongoing, continuous improvement approach as compared to business process reengineering which can be viewed as a one-time change.
2. Gain top management's commitment. Continuous improvement requires ongoing support.
3. Build a multi-discipline team for the project- one that understands lean supply chain management.
4. Analyze the total supply chain process, not just the outbound part or just the inbound part.

Map the process

1. Assess for gaps or redundancies that create time, the key waste.
2. Avoid cannibalizing the process, such as focusing on warehousing or transportation or other activities instead of studying the entire supply chain process.
3. Realize cause-effect impacts. High freight cost, for example, can be a problem or a

symptom. Inventory can be a problem or, more often, a symptom of a problem.

4. Drive for root causes, not symptoms.
5. Ask customers about how well your supply chain operates. Since the supply chain is built on customer pull, the end user has a vital view.
6. Comprehend the complexity of supply chains with multiple suppliers, distribution centres and customers.
7. Appreciate the fundamental impact of international sourcing and shipping on time and inventory.
8. Use event management and exception management to add management and control. Supply chain complexity increases the need for event and exception management technology and capability.
9. Grasp the impact of the organization and culture on supply chain process design and operation.
10. Analyze the effect of continuing external events, such as with Homeland Security for imports, on lead times and on lean dynamics.

Calculate the risks of the lean supply chain

1. Mitigate risks in the redesign.
2. Assess where standardization is feasible and where customizing to specific customers requirements is needed.
3. Collaborate with suppliers. It is a requirement, not an option; and it is a two-way exchange.
4. Demand supplier performance. It is vital to a lean supply chain operation.

5. Measure the present process as total cycle time, costs and inventory (both in dollars and units) and the inventory turns.
6. Integrate the supply chain. Breaks in the flow, both internal and external, can be pockets of waste.
7. Identify non-value added activities, their effect and their cause.
8. Rationalize the process.
9. Improve the process to drive change.
10. Streamline the process for unnecessary complexity and unnecessary suppliers and service providers.
11. Know that technology cannot overcome process flaws.
12. Involve your people-employees, suppliers, service providers to provide input on present supply chain effectiveness and for improvements.
13. Incorporate technology, such as supply chain execution technology, as part of the process improvement. It is an enabler. Understand where standard ERP and other software may and may not enable a lean supply chain.
14. Make the supply chain visible; recognize that blind spots can be areas of waste.
15. Recognize the viability of outsourcing as a driver of needed changes.
16. Probe for uncertainties that create inventory and other waste. Forecasting accuracy is one area of opportunity.
17. Investigate reasons why product does not flow in a more consistent and predictable manner. Order and shipment releases from

suppliers, for example, can create inbound flows that can mitigate time and inventory buffers.

18. Position inventories at the proper distribution centres. The right inventory at the wrong facility can result in inter-facility transfers that add time and extra transport costs and can delay customer order deliveries. This is a non-value added action that generates waste.

19. Be open to the changes of a lean supply chain. From technology, such as RFID, to a completely redesigned process, significant change can be expected.

20. Include change management in your lean program requirements.

Lean supply chain management is not about "fixing" what someone else is doing wrong. It is about identifying and eliminating waste as measured in time, inventory and cost across the complete supply chain. This requires continuous effort and improvement.

A lean supply chain can take reduce time by 10 to 40%, inventories by 10% to 30% and costs by 10% to 25%. Continuous improvements can take payback to the upper range-and beyond. This is a significant benefit to ROI and to the bottom line.

Chapter 17: Connecting Strategy to Supply Chain

Going from business strategy development to creating tangible competitive advantages is a long journey, because no strategy, however brilliant, produces results unless executed.

Therefore, to be useful, a strategy must be implemented. This means that the strategy that establishes the business goals, through which competitive advantage will be created must then be expanded to articulate actions that will take the business toward its strategic goals. This whole process can be thought of as consisting of three basic steps:

1. Strategy development, that is, the process of evaluating the internal and external imperatives, analyzing the industry, products, and customers, and defining an overriding principle of how the company will try to grow. This is equivalent to defining the "what" and "why" of the problem.

2. Strategy planning is the process of assessing the current state of the corporation and evaluating various alternatives that can be potentially considered to achieve the stated imperatives of the business strategy. This step consists of analysis, evaluation, articulation, and prioritization of these alternatives, in effect defining the "how" of the problem.

3. Strategy implementation is the process of starting and managing the individual projects to implement the favoured alternative from step two.

While most companies have some level of formally defined process for developing a business strategy (step 1 above) and an ongoing slew of projects (step 3 above) creating new capabilities and enhancing existing ones, most do not have a formal process for the activities identified in the strategy planning step.

The planning phase focus on gap-image assessment of a firm's business capabilities, therefore determining what must be done; strategy execution emphasizes the actual execution activities, program management, project management, change management, communication, training, and all other organizational aspects for successful execution. While that is important, the intermediate analysis provided by strategy planning is the missing link in most modern corporations in any recognizable formal fashion. In absence of this planning step, corporations fail to establish and prioritize the execution efforts that are aligned with the goals of the business strategy, and fail to identify and prioritize the filling of specific capability gaps.

This middle step of strategy planning is what I call functional strategy. This is the step where firms must assess their business capabilities and determine (1) what capabilities they must build that are aligned to their business strategy and (2) how they must build them to create differentiators to create competitive advantage. This is where the business functions such as supply chain fit-in. This is where a firm needs to assess their current and required supply-chain capabilities to identify the gaps and prioritize their investments in building those missing capabilities.

Joining the business strategy to the functional strategy by assessing your supply-chain capabilities is the key to building successful supply chains. The final piece of execution is what I call deployment strategy falls into place when real projects enabling specific process are planned, budgeted, spun off, and executed. Understanding this continuum from the business strategy to functional to deployment is key to successfully creating competitive advantages to support your business objectives.

Chapter 18: New Supply Chain Design Imperative

Designing effective supply chains is based on recognizing the two basic facts about designing supply chain strategy.

1. Supply chains can only manage demand, supply, inventory, and resources. Therefore, any strategy mandating supply chains to do anything else is not going to help. The supply chain driver is largely determined by the characteristics of the industry, products, and customers. The combinations of these attributes establish the basic nature and constraints of the supply chain capability requirements and therefore, it is largely not an option to be selected.

2. Supply chains exist only to support a business; therefore, a supply chain strategy must subordinate to the business strategy. This means that supply chain strategy cannot be designed in a vacuum, but must be aligned with an explicit business strategy. This is an explicit choice on behalf of the business and depends on the business model that a firm wants to pursue.

The business strategy driver helps in designing the main supply chain process orientation; for example, a cost-driven business will drive supply chain processes designed for asset-efficiency and high resource-utilization. The supply chain driver helps in designing how the exceptions will be handled within the supply chains; what happens when supplies don't match demand, or enough inventories don't exist within the network. Together, these drivers help design processes that match the organizational business objectives while simultaneously addressing the operational needs. And that together creates competitive advantage.

For example, if you selected a demand driven supply chain with cost as business strategy, you would be designing processes with the intent of creating operational efficiencies while a supply chain with inventory as a driver and differentiation as the business strategy will focus on processes to provide flexibility in quick inventory deployments within the network.

Design imperative, is a concept, for designing effective supply chain strategy and building processes that create competitive advantages aligned with the needs of the business strategy of the firm that is the basic theme of leveraging supply chains as an asset. While the conventional supply chain strategies will give you all the buzz-words, it is only through understanding the business goals and operational requirements, that you can actually build a supply chain strategy that is effective.

Looking for an alternate way to design effective supply chains?

The answer does not lie in adopting theories in the hope of finding the right answer, but to build your own supply chain capabilities driven by your business strategy. To find this new approach to build effective supply chains, understand the supply chain sphere of influence, find out what drives your supply chain and the new design imperative to build supply chain capabilities that directly support your business strategies.

Chapter 19: What Drives Your Supply Chain?

The objective of presenting the supply chain's sphere of influence was to establish a very basic, though often missed, fact that supply chains can directly affect only these four components that they directly control. Therefore, any strategy we formulate for supply chain design must directly establish the behaviour of one or more of these four components. Of course, one of these four components must be identified as the primary driver to resolve plan conflicts and to establish the pecking order among the supply chain processes.

Which one of the four components should ideally drive the supply chain in a firm? Should it be demand, supply, inventory, or resources? The answer depends on a number of factors. The industry segment, types of products, attributes of demand, attributes of supply, and finally, the selected business strategy are all factors that need to be analyzed to answer the question of what must drive a supply chain.

A grocery firm with cost as the business strategy will have a dramatically different supply chain compared to that of a grocery store that selects differentiation as its business strategy. Both supply chains will have some common characteristics because they are both in the same industry segment (retail, grocery). For example, they will both require the ability to replenish their stores frequently for fresh produce and perishables; they will both have to develop temperature controlled distribution capabilities, and so on. However, the grocer with differentiation as its business strategy may decide to differentiate itself by developing a supply chain for its produce that tracks its whole life cycle from the farm-to-the-shelf and provides this visibility to the customers to verify the claims of freshness, organic growth, sustainable farming, fair labour, or any similar differentiators that the customers may pay for. While development and maintenance of such capabilities will add supply chain costs for this grocer, it would also create a passionate and loyal customer base for them. In contrast, the supply chain capabilities for the grocer with the cost-based strategy may simply focus on more traditional ways of sourcing from the cheapest suppliers, optimizing inventories and shipping costs, and discounting products near their expiration dates.

The differentiation based business strategy, therefore, drives its own requirements for the supply chain capabilities that are different from those of the cost based business strategy, while both the firms must also have a basic set of common capabilities. In this example, what is driving the two supply chains? While both of the grocery retailers need to be demand-driven, the one with differentiation as their business strategy must balance this against the supply driven aspects, simply because they will have to manage many more constraints on the supply side, controlling quality through the assortment they carry, the sourcing that must support their policy of freshness, fair labour practices, organic fertilizers, and so on.

Unlike the current strategies that tend to conclude that the supply chain must be lean or agile, speculation or postponement-oriented, thinking through the core sphere of supply chain influence generally points to a process group belonging to one of the four components, which becomes the focus for creating competitive capabilities. This allows a specific guidance from the strategy to design, rather than providing a high-level general directive of being lean or agile.

By process group, I mean the collective supply chain processes that are used to manage any one of the four components of the supply chain sphere of influence. In the example of the two grocers, the grocer with the cost-based business strategy will likely focus on inventory and resource process groups to leverage cost advantages, while the grocer with the differentiation business strategy will focus on supply process group. Remember though that these process groups only identify where the firm has the most potential to create advantages, even though they will have to develop capabilities in all process groups that bring them up to par with the competitors.

In this view of supply chain strategy, one of the four core spheres of influence is identified to be the primary sphere. This helps the firm identify where they can derive the most competitive advantages and operate optimally. For example, the demand-driven supply chain will evaluate all alternatives in response to a change with the view of minimizing their impact on the demand plans; a supply-driven supply chain will do the same to minimize their impact on the supply plans, and so on.

Retail supply chains are great examples of demand-driven supply chains. Examples for supply-driven supply chains would be in industries where supplies are limited or controlled tightly by a small set of suppliers for example, Toyota's manufacturing plant in China making batteries for their hybrids that needs rare-earths which are controlled by the Chinese government. Resource driven supply chains are those where the resource skills are rare or capital costs are high (requiring very high utilization) or set-up changes very expensive; for example a steel manufacturer with blast furnace whose supply chain will be managed around the furnace utilization and set-up changes. A good example of inventory driven supply-chains will be an airline's maintenance operations where the availability of critical spares for their planes can impact their profitability in a substantial way by keeping their productive assets out of service.

Chapter 20: Speculation as Supply Chain Strategy

The speculation strategy is really based on savings created through economies of scale, by creating and delivering the finished goods in bulk. The speculation strategy reduces the cost of logistics by maximizing the usage of resources like warehouses and trucks, and reduces the cost of manufacturing by running large production batches that improve throughput by reducing the cost of set-up changes and by reducing the raw material costs by buying in bulk. This strategy leverages the large lot-sizes to produce the economies of scale in manufacturing and distribution, but it is prone to having higher inventory costs due to higher inventory levels and obsolescence.

As speculation strategy is based on creating economies of scale through mass production and distribution, the supply chain processes based on this strategy generally create stable plans without much volatility. The low volatility in plans does not require highly responsive supply chain design, especially when compared to the supply chains that cater to a postponement strategy.

However, just as postponement was more of a business model and less of a supply chain choice, the same is true for speculation. The ability to leverage economies of scale or speculation is not a choice: It is an imperative imposed by the type of industry, assortment, and demand patterns. Consider, for example, an assemble-to-order manufacturer such as custom-built gaming machines must adopt postponement, because the speculation strategy will simply produce too many unwanted machines, making the business model unfeasible. In real-life businesses, the business model, dependent on industry, products, and demand patterns, forces a business model that is either speculative in nature or allows for postponement. The business model pursued then casts the requirements for a supply chain that must simply support the business. Therefore postponement or speculation remains a strategy for business and not something open for the supply chain to ponder upon and pursue.

The situations in which speculation or postponement is an explicit choice to be made for a supply chain are limited, but may become real options for specific categories of products or sales channels of a company. For example, consider Dell with their new business model to sell through the retail stores. In the changed scenario, Dell must master a speculation model of supply chain to fill the retail channels with prebuilt machines, but they can continue to use their postponement model of supply chain design to effectively build machines for their online sales of computers.

Chapter 21: Postponement as Supply Chain Strategy

The postponement strategy is based on the following two basic principles of demand forecasting.

1. The accuracy of the forecast demand decreases with an increase in the time horizon. The further the time window for which the demand is being forecasted, the more inaccurate it will be. As time extends further into the future, the forecast error grows, showing that the forecast demand will have larger and larger variations as time periods progress into the future.

2. Demand projections for a product group are generally more accurate than projections for individual products. For example, it is much easier to forecast the total demand for LCD TVs than it is for an individual TV of a specific brand, model, screen size, resolution, and colour contrast ratio.

The postponement strategy leverages the above characteristics of demand forecasting. It dictates that the firms should postpone the creation or delivery of the final product as long as possible. For retailers, this takes the shape of postponing the delivery of the final product to its destination, while for assemble-to-order manufacturers this means postponing the final assembly of the product. For manufacturing scenarios like build-to-stock, the postponement strategy may drive pushing the packaging or final assembly of the products, allowing the manufacturer to personalize, configure finished products to customer orders, and change the final product mix to suit any changes in demand. The postponement strategy effectively reduces inventory obsolescence and takes out the risk and uncertainty costs associated with having undesirable products, but it requires an integrated and agile supply chain to ensure that the latest demand forecasts can be frequently created and propagated through the supply chain to produce or allocate the right products for their customers.

While postponement is conventionally thought of as a supply chain strategy, a little thinking will dispel this notion. Postponement is not an absolute choice, it is an imperative forced by the type of industry, assortment, and demand patterns. For example, a postponement strategy for delivering supplies to a trauma centre or cereal to a grocery store are just not practical choices, even though it may allow for delivery of specific medical kits optimal for the type of trauma or the correct size of cereal packages in response to the actual demand. Therefore, medical supplies manufacturer cannot select postponement as their supply chain strategy any more than a grocer can postpone delivering their cereal. However, in few situations the production and demand patterns may allow postponement to become a business option, in which case, the supply chain must be designed to support that choice; an example is Avon. Avon declined to label their bottles themselves for a long time, viewing this as additional cost and complexity.

However, after developing an end-to-end supply chain visibility, Avon saw the opportunity in postponing the creation of its final product by placing the labels in the desired target language. It successfully deployed an idea that had been pushed out earlier, after understanding that this allowed them to postpone the production of final finished goods and better align their supplies to the end-demand without tremendously increasing their inventory.

The situations in which postponement may be an explicit choice to be made for a supply chain are limited, but may become real options for specific categories of products or sales channels of a company. For example, Dell has mastered the art of postponement for their custom-designed machines for individual consumers. When Dell started, this was not necessarily the case in the industry, however, Dell invented a new business model and leveraged postponement as a business model not as a supply chain strategy; though, it then designed their supply chain to support this business model. That is the distinction I want to make clear; postponement as a business model which then drives the supply chain strategy and not the other way around. And that is also the reason for why I believe that postponement as a supply chain strategy puts the facts on their head – supply chain strategy must follow a business strategy and not the other way around!

Chapter 22: Lean and Agile Supply Chain at the Same Time.

The fact is that most of the supply chains need to be lean and agile simultaneously. After all you can't have a lean supply chain that is cost-effective but is unable to react to any changes or an agile supply chain that is good at responding to changes but simply unsustainable financially.

Wal-Mart is a prime example: Their explicitly stated business strategy of low prices has driven them to consistently reduce their cost of operations through supply chain innovations. Wal-Mart's supply chain is definitely among the most cost-efficient in the industry. However, it is also quite agile. Wal-Mart was the only major retailer to reorient their assortment with national colours and substantially increase their American flag-based merchandise after the 9/11 attacks in a very short time. Absence of any major clearance at their stores also points to an agile supply chain that can adapt itself quickly to changes, thereby avoiding overstocked stores and the need to discount merchandise to clear the shelves.

How can a supply chain be both lean and agile at the same time?

A firm can regard both lean and agile strategies as process drivers for designing individual supply chain processes rather than as being all-encompassing strategies for developing a supply chain as a whole. In this context, they become the principles that practitioners can use to develop standard processes that leverage one of these attributes even as process exceptions leverages the other. For example, a firm may establish a store-based inventory policy using the lean principle to cover the supply lead-time from the primary warehouse to the store. While the lean design drives their standard replenishment to the store, the process to handle exceptions to manage stock-outs may leverage agile principles, allowing priority replenishments to the store from a set of alternate sources in order to avoid losing substantial sales revenues. The example of Wal-Mart illustrates the complementary use of lean and agile design principles in designing a supply chain that is highly effective while Wal-Mart uses inventory optimization and transportation optimization processes to reduce the costs (lean), it also uses cross-docking to actively respond to the latest store demand (agile).

Therefore, the question of whether a supply chain should be lean or agile becomes rhetorical. Any large enterprise cannot have a rigidly designed supply chain that is either lean or agile. Both of these aspects of lean and agile are required in designing an effective supply chain to support the business.

Chapter 23: Agile as Supply Chain Strategy

Agile refers to the ability to react and adapt to the changes in demand and supply situations in a supply chain. To accommodate the inherent variations in demand and supply, supply chains need to react and adapt to such changes as they happen, to minimize the disruption and optimize the objectives, such as costs, fulfilment rates, inventory, and so on. So what does it mean to have an agile supply chain?

An agile supply chain design will have redundancy built into its processes, allowing it to quickly respond to expected changes. This supply chain will be best to maximize the service levels for fulfilling demand, manufacturing personalized products, and providing excellent customer service. These objectives will drive the supply chain to keep higher levels of inventories to maintain order fulfilment targets, favour on-time deliveries over cheaper shipments, and favour quality inputs and personalized services over mass produced, commoditized goods. These supply chains will have more flexible supplier contracts that enable them to change order quantities, destinations, need dates, and even cancel the orders altogether if the demand falls off a cliff. Suppliers will typically allow such flexibility for a cost.

When demand suddenly rises and the primary suppliers cannot cope with the increased demand, an agile supply chain will go to a secondary set of suppliers that would have been established in advance for maintaining supplies for such an eventuality. As purchase volumes for the secondary suppliers will be low and demand uneven, the costs of such contracts is generally higher. However, having all these layers of extra inventories, warehousing, transportation, and suppliers will provide enough buffer to the supply chain to handle most variations in demand, supply, or lead-time while maintaining its stated service levels.

Contrast this supply chain with the one based on lean as the driving principle and you will notice the contrasts.

Agile supports the natural designs of supply chain which exist to manage variability. However, the extent of variability in the demand, lead-time, and operations must determine the amount of agility (and hence the amount of redundancy) designed into the supply chain.

Also, most firms have a large assortment of material to be managed: Raw materials, WIP, finished goods, and retail assortments almost always consist of a mixed bag of products when it comes to their demand profile. Some of these products may have a stable demand profile, while others will be more volatile. This means that the enterprise supply chain that must be designed to cater to all these types of products must be lean (to best manage the products with a stable demand) and agile (to manage others with volatile demand) simultaneously. After all, you could not run a business with a lean supply chain with the lowest cost, but that cannot respond to any changes in demand or supply. Since all demand and supply has inherent variability, such a rigidly designed supply chain will quickly build up unwanted and obsolete inventories as it is incapable of reacting to changes in demand and supply. To the same extent, one also cannot run a supply chain that is extremely responsive and manages the changes in demand and supplies precisely, because such a supply chain will have an unreasonably high cost to operate, quickly running out of working capital to support daily operations.

Therefore, I see both of these attributes as core capabilities of any supply chain design, being complementary rather than being exclusive to each other.

Chapter 24: Supply Chain Area of Influence

Till now, we have discussed the most common of the supply chain strategies: lean, agile, speculation, and postponement. In doing so, we also highlighted the underlying concepts behind each of these so-called strategies and why they fail to deliver as supply chain strategies.

All supply chains have a core sphere of influence that does not change irrespective of the industry or products or customers. Therefore, a generic supply chain strategy must be formulated within this context. Manipulating the supply chain area of influence leads to defining the generic supply chain strategies. Supply chains directly manage the following four basic components of a firm's value chain: Which I call the supply chain area of influence.

Management of demand:

While the end consumer demand is an independent variable, once the finished goods demand has been forecast, it is the supply chain processes that propagate the demand along the supply chain nodes. As the demand propagates through the network, supply chain processes may determine the optimal way to fulfil this demand, including where, when, and how this will happen. For the manufacturing supply chains, this propagation will take the demand to the warehouses, then to the assembly plants and factories,

103

and finally to the raw material warehouses and vendors. Along the way, the finished goods demand will be broken down into its subassemblies, components, and raw materials using a bill of materials, as well as into its manufacturing operations and resources, using the bills of routing and resources. For retail supply chains, the propagation process will take the demand to its warehouses and then to the suppliers. Thus, while the end demand may be independent, the supply chain processes have a huge impact in managing demand through propagation and determining the fulfilment methods throughout the supply network.

Management of supply:

As the demand is propagated from the customer end to the supply end of the supply chain, the replenishment planning processes start creating the fulfilment plans, which results in an opposite propagation of supply to fulfil the demand at every node for every finished product, work-in-progress (WIP), or raw material. The replenishment plans finally drive the procurement process that replenishes the supply chain inventories from the firm's suppliers. Supplies from the vendors are managed through purchasing and logistics to replenish the supply chain nodes from where the supply propagation continues toward the demand end. These processes of demand and supply planning must work in concert for a smoothly run supply chain. Managing supply with demand is the most important function of a supply chain and since neither demand nor supply is static, the agility with which they are planned and replanned differentiates one supply chain from another.

Management of inventory:

This is the third part of the puzzle that supply chains directly control. Inventories make it possible for the supply chains to react to the changes in supply and demand while simultaneously maintaining acceptable fulfilment rates. However, inventories add cost that directly comes from the working capital of a company and therefore, needs to be reduced as far as possible while protecting the ability of the supply chain to service the demand. Supply chain processes of inventory classification and inventory planning help the corporations achieve that balance. The quality of the inventory planning processes depends on the underlying science, accuracy of historical and forecasted demand, supply and lead-time data, and cost models for inventory. The results of this process directly affect the leanness of a supply chain by affecting inventory costs and affect agility by maintaining demand fulfilment targets under varying conditions of demand and supply.

Management of resources:

This is the last component of the corporate operations directly affected by supply chain processes. It is also the most complex and wide in scope since resources encompass so much in a corporation; they are the people, machinery, warehouses, trucks, forklifts, conveyors, and so on. A lot of these resources enable supply chain processes in the corporate offices, warehouses, factories, ports, in-transit, and stores. Supply chain processes create resource plans and affect the efficiency and utilization of these resources. Throughput in a warehouse or factory is a direct result of efficient planning and scheduling capabilities. In a wider definition, one could consider inventory and cash as resources as well. We chose to consider inventory separately since there are very specific supply chain processes addressing inventory planning. Cash is a legitimate resource for a corporation and even though supply chains impact it through working capital (inventory and operations), receivables, and payables (cash-to-cash cycles), we do not consider this in the primary area of influence of the physical supply chain. The reason to do so is that while supply chain capabilities impact the financial results, they do not manipulate cash as they manage the other components of inventory, demand, supply, and resources.

Chapter 25: Essential Elements of Supply Chain Management

Collaborative Product Life Cycle Management

The objective is to share relevant information with appropriate partners and enlist their expertise in design activities at the earliest possible time in Product Life Cycle Management (PLM).

Emphasis is to acquire and apply the skills, knowledge, and experience of your extended enterprise to develop the products that best serve customer needs at low cost in a short cycle time.

Demand Planning

Objective is to provide the entire extended supply chain network with the demand planning information needed for optimum planning and schedule execution.

Emphasis is on accurate and real time, collaborative demand planning to support production and supply chain execution.

Supply Source Planning

Objective is to optimize projected customer demand with supply source planning through Collaborative Planning, Forecasting and Replenishment (CPFR) and subsequent schedule execution by supplier partners.

Emphasis is on compatibility of collaborative business process and precise and timely communications to minimize non-performance risk.

Schedule Execution

Objective is to make reliable, short-cycle, capable-to-promise schedules and achieve100% schedule performance.

Emphasis is on schedule reliability and responsiveness to planned demand and unforeseen changes in demand.

Logistics Management

Objective is to optimally deliver product to customers as promised while minimizing logistics costs.

Emphasis is on warehouse and transportation management systems that efficiently plan and control the movement of goods while continually seeking to lower logistics costs.

Event Management

Objective is to proactively monitor and trigger signals about undesirable events requiring action somewhere in the supply chain. In addition, logic may exist that will identify opportunities to minimize costs and increase customer service.

Emphasis is on preventing internal and external problems that are likely to interrupt material flow by sending alert messages to the first level and escalating the alert signal up the organization until the alert is shut down.

Throughout the supply chain, there are some absolutely critical and predictive event questions your system should accurately and quickly answer:

1. When will specific orders really ship?
2. Which orders will be late?
3. Why will these orders be late?
4. What are the specific problems that are delaying the schedule?
5. What are the future schedule problems and when will they occur?
6. What is the best schedule that can be executed now?

If management can accurately answer predictive questions, decision quality will greatly improve. Preventive actions can offset what were once unforeseen events. The supply chain will be managed more effectively and improve your chances of gaining a competitive advantage.

Chapter 26: Impacts of Inventory Control in Supply Chain Management

Inventory Control: Improving the Bottom Line

Inventory control requires the tracking of all parts and materials purchased, products processed, and products stored and ready for shipment. Having a sophisticated tracking system alone does not improve your bottom line, it is how you use the information that your system provides.

If your job responsibilities involve inventory control, you know how critical the function is to business success and the complexities involved in planning, executing and controlling your supply chain network.

From a financial perspective, inventory control is no small matter. Oftentimes, inventory is the largest asset item on a manufacturer's or distributor's balance sheet. As a result, there is a lot of management emphasis on keeping inventories down so they do not consume too much cash. The objectives of inventory reduction and minimization are more easily accomplished with modern inventory management processes that are working effectively.

Inventory Control Problems

In actual practice the vast majority of manufacturing and distribution companies suffer from lower customer service, higher costs and excessive inventories than are necessary. Inventory control problems are usually the result of using poor processes, practices and antiquated support systems. The inventory management process is much more complex than the uninitiated understand. In fact, in many companies the inventory control department is perceived as little more than a clerical function. When this is the case, the fact is the function is probably not very effective.

The likely result of this approach to inventory control is lots of material shortages, excessive inventories, high costs and poor customer service. For example, if a customer orders a product that requires a manufacturer to acquire 20 part numbers to assemble a product and then, only 19 of the 20 part numbers are available, you have nineteen part numbers which are excess inventory. Worse, the product can't be shipped to create revenue and the customer is not serviced. Think for a moment about the complexities of making products that require hundreds and maybe thousands of part numbers to be available in the right quantity, at the right place and at the right time to make products to satisfy customer orders. It is a complex network to control and a set of inventory management tasks that must be performed with precision.

What Should Be Done?

Too much inventory and not high enough customer service is very common, but unnecessary. There are proven methods that can help you accurately project customer demand and to calculate the inventory you will need to meet your defined level of customer service. Using the right techniques for sales forecasting and inventory management will allow you to monitor changes and respond to alerts when action needs to be taken. The right approach to inventory control can produce dramatic benefits in customer service with lower inventory, no matter how complex your network is.

Modern inventory management processes utilize new and more refined techniques that provide for dynamic optimization of inventories to maximize customer service with decreased inventory and lower costs. These improved approaches to inventory management are of major consequence to overall competitiveness where the highest level of customer service and delivered value can favourably impact market share and profits.

Understanding the Process

Overall inventory control crosses a number of functions. The inventory control process can be divided into the following general categories. Demand management which covers the processes for sales and operations planning, sales forecasting and finished goods inventory deployment planning.

1. Inventory planning and ordering which is often accomplished with material requirements planning, often referred to by its acronym MRP or in a lean manufacturing environment kanban ordering is used to effect deliveries of material.

2. Inventory optimization systems are being advocated by some as the supply chain management mechanism that should be used to mathematically calculate where inventory should be deployed to satisfy predetermined supply chain management objectives.

3. Physical inventory control is a phrase that describes the receiving, movement, stocking and overall physical control of inventories.

Effective inventory control is a vital function to help insure the success of manufacturing and distribution companies. The effectiveness of inventory control is directly measurable by how successful a company is in providing high levels of customer service, low inventory investment, maximum throughput and low costs. Certainly, an area where management should apply a philosophy of aggressive improvement.

Inventory Management: Improving Profit Performance

A truly effective inventory management system will minimize the complexities involved in planning, executing and controlling a supply chain network which is critical to business success. The opportunities available by improving a company's inventory management can significantly improve bottom line business performance.

From a financial perspective, inventory management is no small matter. Oftentimes, inventory is the largest asset item on a manufacturer's or distributor's balance sheet. As a result, there is a lot of management emphasis on keeping inventories down so they do not consume too much cash. The objectives of inventory reduction and minimization are more easily accomplished with modern inventory management processes that are working effectively.

Chapter 27: Benefits of Supply Chain

The importance of Supply Chain Management is to:
1. Reduced inventories along the chain.
2. Better information sharing among the partners.
3. Planning being done in consultation rather than in isolation.

The benefits too would be reflected in terms of:
1. Lower costs.
2. Better customer service.
3. Efficient manufacturing.
4. Better trust among the partners leading to win-win.

Process integration and other efforts result in improved quality as higher profit margins shall get reflected in creation of better facilities for manufacturing, product design research, and enhanced customer service.

Supply chains, no doubt, are expensive and complicated at times. Yet because they leverage the overall efforts of reaching out to the ultimate customers in a cost effective and smooth manner that they have real benefit to have one or many.

There could be a situation where a supplier may satisfy the ultimate customer directly, for example a vegetable vendor reaching out to his customer by the road side.

This may not need any supply chain to work but suppose the same supplier meeting the needs of many customers spread along the length and the width of his city, needing vegetable around the same time. Obviously, they may need one or many delivery outlets from the supplier, some stocking by the supplier and thus a small but suitable warehouse by the supplier.

Supply chains exist to overcome the gaps created when suppliers are distance away from the customers. They help in conducting operations that can be done only at a distance from the customers.

Benefit of supply chain can be understood by a simple imagination of a service that passes through various modes, covering various regions to finally reach the ultimate customers needing that service in yet another and various locations. It involves moving materials in geographically separate locations and meeting usually a mismatched demand of that material.

For example, let us say that a firm operating from four factories has to supply materials to eight customers. If all the factories supply to all the customers directly then there would be in all 32 routes!

However, if all the materials from the 4 factories are offloaded in a warehouse that caters to the need of the 8 customers then only 4 inward and 8 outbound routes , that is 4+8 = 12 routes shall be required.

A well designed supply chain shall provide the following benefits:

1. Operations can be located in the best locations irrespective of customers' locations.
2. Bigger facilities can be created and hence economies of scale can be thought of.
3. Large stocks need not be kept at the producer's end as the same can be kept with wholesalers near the customers.
4. Retailers carry less stock as whole sellers provide them the materials whenever needed.
5. Lead times for retailers are short.
6. Uninterrupted availability to customers.
7. Transport is simpler and routine.

Chapter 28: Supply Chain Epoch

Creation era

The term supply chain management was first coined by Keith Oliver in 1982. However, the concept of a supply chain in management was of great importance long before, in the early 20th century, especially with the creation of the assembly line. The characteristics of this era of supply chain management include the need for large-scale changes, re-engineering, downsizing driven by cost reduction programs, and widespread attention to the Japanese practice of management.

Integration era

This era of supply chain management studies was highlighted with the development of Electronic Data Interchange (EDI) systems in the 1960s and developed through the 1990s by the introduction of Enterprise Resource Planning (ERP) systems. This era has continued to develop into the 21st century with the expansion of internet-based collaborative systems. This era of supply chain evolution is characterized by both increasing value-adding and cost reductions through integration.

In fact a supply chain can be classified as a Stage 1, 2 or 3 networks. In stage 1 type supply chain, various systems such as Make, Storage, Distribution, Material control, etc. are not linked and are independent of each other. In a stage 2 supply chain, these are integrated under one plan and are ERP enabled. A stage 3 supply chain is one in which vertical integration with the suppliers in upstream direction and customers in downstream direction are achieved. An example of this kind of supply chain is Amazon.

Globalization era

The third movement of supply chain management development, the globalization era, can be characterized by the attention given to global systems of supplier relationships and the expansion of supply chains over national boundaries and into other continents. Although the use of global sources in the supply chain of organizations can be traced back several decades (e.g., in the oil industry), it was not until the late 1980s that a considerable number of organizations started to integrate global sources into their core business. This era is characterized by the globalization of supply chain management in organizations with the goal of increasing their competitive advantage, value-adding, and reducing costs through global sourcing.

Specialization era

Outsourced manufacturing and distribution

In the 1990s, industries began to focus on "core competencies" and adopted a specialization model. Companies abandoned vertical integration, sold off non-core operations, and outsourced those functions to other companies. This changed management requirements by extending the supply chain well beyond company walls and distributing management across specialized supply chain partnerships.

This transition also re-focused the fundamental perspectives of each respective organization. OEMs became brand owners that needed deep visibility into their supply base. They had to control the entire supply chain from above instead of from within. Contract manufacturers had to manage bills of material with different part numbering schemes from multiple OEMs and support customer requests for work-in-process visibility and vendor-managed inventory (VMI).

The specialization model creates manufacturing and distribution networks composed of multiple, individual supply chains specific to products, suppliers, and customers, who work together to design, manufacture, distribute, market, sell, and service a product. The set of partners may change according to a given market, region, or channel, resulting in a proliferation of trading partner environments, each with its own unique characteristics and demands.

Supply chain management as a service

Specialization within the supply chain began in the 1980s with the inception of transportation brokerages, warehouse management, and non-asset-based carriers and has matured beyond transportation and logistics into aspects of supply planning, collaboration, execution and performance management.

At any given moment, market forces could demand changes from suppliers, logistics providers, locations and customers, and from any number of these specialized participants as components of supply chain networks. This variability has significant effects on the supply chain infrastructure, from the foundation layers of establishing and managing the electronic communication between the trading partners to more complex requirements including the configuration of the processes and work flows that are essential to the management of the network itself.

Supply chain specialization enables companies to improve their overall competencies in the same way that outsourced manufacturing and distribution has done; it allows them to focus on their core competencies and assemble networks of specific, best-in-class partners to contribute to the overall value chain itself, thereby increasing overall performance and efficiency. The ability to quickly obtain and deploy this domain-specific supply chain expertise without developing and maintaining an entirely unique and complex competency in house is the leading reason why supply chain specialization is gaining popularity.

Chapter 29: Supply Chain Management 2.0

Outsourced technology hosting for supply chain solutions debuted in the late 1990s and has taken root primarily in transportation and collaboration categories. This has progressed from the Application Service Provider (ASP) model from approximately 1998 through 2003 to the On-Demand model from approximately 2003-2006 to the Software as a Service (SaaS) model currently in focus today.

Building on globalization and specialization, the term SCM 2.0 has been coined to describe both the changes within the supply chain itself as well as the evolution of the processes, methods and tools that manage it in this new "era".

Web 2.0 is defined as a trend in the use of the World Wide Web that is meant to increase creativity, information sharing, and collaboration among users. At its core, the common attribute that Web 2.0 brings is to help navigate the vast amount of information available on the Web in order to find what is being sought. It is the notion of a usable pathway. SCM 2.0 follows this notion into supply chain operations. It is the pathway to SCM results, a combination of the processes, methodologies, tools and delivery options to guide companies to their results quickly as the complexity and speed of the supply chain increase due to the effects of global competition, rapid price fluctuations, surging oil prices, short product life cycles, expanded specialization, near-/far- and off-shoring, and talent scarcity.

SCM 2.0 leverages proven solutions designed to rapidly deliver results with the ability to quickly manage future change for continuous flexibility, value and success. This is delivered through competency networks composed of best-of-breed supply chain domain expertise to understand which elements, both operationally and organizationally, are the critical few that deliver the results as well as through intimate understanding of how to manage these elements to achieve desired results.

Finally, the solutions are delivered in a variety of options, such as no-touch via business process outsourcing, mid-touch via managed services and software as a service (SaaS), or high touch in the traditional software deployment model.

Business process integration

Successful SCM requires a change from managing individual functions to integrating activities into key supply chain processes. An example scenario: the purchasing department places orders as requirements become known. The marketing department, responding to customer demand, communicates with several distributors and retailers as it attempts to determine ways to satisfy this demand. Information shared between supply chain partners can only be fully leveraged through process integration.

Supply chain business process integration involves collaborative work between buyers and suppliers, joint product development, common systems and shared information in the following areas.

1. Customer service management process

Customer Relationship Management concerns the relationship between the organization and its customers. Customer service is the source of customer information. It also provides the customer with real-time information on scheduling and product availability through interfaces with the company's production and distribution operations. Successful organizations use the following steps to build customer relationships:

1. Determine mutually satisfying goals for organization and customers.
2. Establish and maintain customer rapport.
3. Produce positive feelings in the organization and the customers.

2. Procurement process

Strategic plans are drawn up with suppliers to support the manufacturing flow management process and the development of new products. In firms where operations extend globally, sourcing should be managed on a global basis. The desired outcome is a win-win relationship where both parties benefit, and a reduction in time required for the design cycle and product development. Also, the purchasing function develops rapid communication systems, such as electronic data interchange (EDI) and Internet linkage to convey possible requirements more rapidly. Activities related to obtaining products and materials from outside suppliers involve resource planning, supply sourcing, negotiation, order placement, inbound transportation, storage, handling and quality assurance, many of which include the responsibility to coordinate with suppliers on matters of scheduling, supply continuity, hedging, and research into new sources or programs.

3. Product development and commercialization

Here, customers and suppliers must be integrated into the product development process in order to reduce time to market. As product life cycles shorten, the appropriate products must be developed and successfully launched with ever shorter time-schedules to remain competitive. Managers of the product development and commercialization process must:

1. Coordinate with customer relationship management to identify customer-articulated needs.
2. Select materials and suppliers in conjunction with procurement.
3. Develop production technology in manufacturing flow to manufacture and integrate into the best supply chain flow for the product/market combination.

4. Manufacturing flow management process

The manufacturing process produces and supplies products to the distribution channels based on past forecasts. Manufacturing processes must be flexible to respond to market changes and must accommodate mass customization. Orders are processes operating on a just-in-time (JIT) basis in minimum lot sizes. Also, changes in the manufacturing flow process lead to shorter cycle times, meaning improved responsiveness and efficiency in meeting customer demand. Activities related to planning, scheduling and supporting manufacturing operations, such as work-in-process storage, handling, transportation, and time phasing of components, inventory at manufacturing sites and maximum flexibility in the coordination of geographic and final assemblies postponement of physical distribution operations.

5. Physical distribution

This concerns movement of a finished product/service to customers. In physical distribution, the customer is the final destination of a marketing channel, and the availability of the product/service is a vital part of each channel participant's marketing effort. It is also through the physical distribution process that the time and space of customer service become an integral part of marketing, thus it links a marketing channel with its customers (e.g., links manufacturers, wholesalers, retailers).

6. Outsourcing/partnerships

This is not just outsourcing the procurement of materials and components, but also outsourcing of services that traditionally have been provided in-house. The logic of this trend is that the company will increasingly focus on those activities in the value chain where it has a distinctive advantage, and outsource everything else. This movement has been particularly evident in logistics where the provision of transport, warehousing and inventory control is increasingly subcontracted to specialists or logistics partners. Also, managing and controlling this network of partners and suppliers requires a blend of both central and local involvement. Hence, strategic decisions need to be taken centrally, with the monitoring and control of supplier performance and day-to-day liaison with logistics partners being best managed at a local level.

7. Performance measurement

Experts found a strong relationship from the largest arcs of supplier and customer integration to market share and profitability. Taking advantage of supplier capabilities and emphasizing a long-term supply chain perspective in customer relationships can both be correlated with firm performance. As logistics competency becomes a more critical factor in creating and maintaining competitive advantage, logistics measurement becomes increasingly important because the difference between profitable and unprofitable operations becomes narrower. According to experts, internal measures are generally collected and analyzed by the firm including

1. Cost
2. Customer Service
3. Productivity measures
4. Asset measurement, and
5. Quality

External performance measurement is examined through customer perception measures and "best practice" benchmarking, and includes 1) customer perception measurement, and 2) best practice benchmarking.

8. Warehousing management

As a case of reducing company cost and expenses, warehousing management is carrying the valuable role against operations. In case of perfect storing and office with all convenient facilities in company level, reducing manpower cost, dispatching authority with on time delivery, loading and unloading facilities with proper area, area for service station, stock management system etc.

Chapter 30: Developing and Implementing Lean Supply Chain

Being able to understanding and identify waste then requires removing that waste. The initial question then is where and how to begin implementing lean supply chain management.

Three points must be recognized. First, lean requires a strategy. It is not just a supply chain program or just a manufacturing program. It is a paradigm that requires a change throughout the organization if it is to be truly successful in removing waste and adding value. Organizations must look at everything differently.

Second, lean goes beyond the four walls of the warehouse or factory. It goes beyond the organizational boundaries of the company and extends to suppliers and to customers. This breadth of scope is why it requires strategy for success.

Third, there are lean principles that must be the basis of the lean supply chain. Namely-
1. Determine value from the view of the customer, not the view of the company.
2. Make the product and information flow.
3. Pull product; do not push it.
4. Manage toward perfection with continuous improvement.

Challenges

Supply chain management, especially developing and implementing lean supply chain management, has challenges that must be acknowledged. These are in addition to the "usual" company issues with lean, such as lack of implementation know-how, resistance to change, lack of a crisis to create urgency, gaining resources and commitment, and back-sliding.

Sometimes these challenges are not addressed or appreciated with lean supply chain management. These include:

1. International sourcing: Procuring finished goods or raw materials in China, India, Brazil and elsewhere outside of your country creates a significant obstacle to lean. The order-to-delivery time is long. Time is a waste, and it compounds the inventory waste issue by making firms buffer and carry more inventory than is needed to compensate for the time. Being lean with a 20-40 day transit time brings a unique test to developing lean supply chain management.

2. Accounting-Standard cost accounting and generally accepted accounting does not recognize waste as lean does. Not having financial support to waste and value identification makes lean difficult to implement and sustain. Inventory and time are not regarded as lean does. Inventory is not an asset for lean. Accounting systems do not

recognize time. Rework is not treated the same with accounting.

3. Organization silos-Supply chain management and lean are processes that cross organization boundaries. Implementing a process that goes horizontal on a vertical and functionally defined organization creates gaps in both processes. These gaps create areas where waste can develop and where removing it can be difficult.

4. Number of firms: There are many suppliers and many logistics service providers in a supply chain. Some of these are visible; some are less visible. Many suppliers or logistics service firms do not practice lean. Taking lean outside the four walls of the company into other firms adds to the time and complexity of implementing and becoming lean.

How to Begin

The initial step to implementing lean is to evaluate and to measure the present supply chain. You have to know where you are to begin the long journey of continuous improvement. Value stream mapping (VSM) is a visual tool to define the current state of a company's supply chain, to identify waste and to lay the foundation in determining the future state flow of the supply chain.

Value stream mapping (VSM) identifies waste in supply chains, especially with regards to time and inventory. Initial VSM efforts include defining the present value stream for product families, those that share common operations or have large volume impact, either units or dollars, or other delineator as determined.

With mapping the current supply chain state, you can then draw on the various lean tools to design the future supply chain flow. This future state should include the infrastructure to support it-training, culture, quality methods, accounting systems, and investment policies.

Lean Tools

There are tools to becoming lean. Each have differences as to ease of use, time to implement, benefits and risk.

5S: The 5S's-Sort, Straighten, Sweep/Shine, Standardize, Sustain/Self-discipline is a visual way to organize to remove waste with extra time for travel or employees. This tool can be used in distribution centres and in offices.

Rapid setup: Rapid setup or changeover has application in the warehouse to adjust layout for seasonal products, new products and changes in what products are fast-moving and often picked and the complementary items that go with these fast-movers. Reducing the time can involve housekeeping and maintenance (including 5S), setting up smaller areas for SKUs, technology (such as warehouse management systems and RFID).

Standardize: Standardize involves efficient work process that are repeatedly followed to define the **who, what, how, where, and when**. This tool helps firms to synchronize the time required to pull and ship all the orders (takt time) and the actual time to do this (cycle time). It can be the basis for employee training. Use of this tool can range from warehouses, issuing purchase orders and other office activities.

Kan-ban: Using kan-ban presents a new, unique way to view "warehousing" and inventory positioning in the supply chain. It presents a way to coordinate multi-step processes for multiple products. With kan-ban, small stocks of inventory are placed in dedicated location(s) for supply chain control. This approach runs counter to the traditional way of large distribution centres delivered truckloads of products to stores or customers. Instead mini-"warehouses" are used to position inventory closer to the end customer and increase the rapidity of delivery and inventory turns. Point of sale and other technologies can be the withdrawal signal to trigger both drawing from and replenishing kan-bans.

Items placed in supply chain kan-bans could be limited to high value inventory, such as "A" items, and then using regular warehouse for the B and C items. A variation to kan-ban is with the import supply chains and differentiating A versus B versus C items and using faster mode and faster carrier transit methods for select items. This reduces time and inventory with smaller batch sizes for these select items. All inventories are not treated the same way from suppliers nor with regards to warehousing.

Workcell: A workcell is a unit larger than an individual operation but smaller than a department. It is self-contained as to equipment and resources. The potential application is with combining multi-operations into a central area exists where warehouse do additional activities, such as kitting or assembly.

6 sigma: This is an advanced tool and ties to quality. The focus is variation and controlling and is preventing errors. Statistical measurement is fundamental. It is used throughout the supply chain, not just in select activities or locations. Six sigma takes lean supply chain management to its ultimate level.

There is no "one" tool for lean supply chain management. Various tools can be used in different areas and in different sequences to add value and reduce waste.

Often, there are complementary or supporting processes with lean supply chain management. The additional processes may include Strategic Sourcing to manage supplier performance for critical and important items; Strategic Customer to gain the needed viewpoint of key customers; and Sales and Operations Planning to blend the strategic sourcing and customer with the tactical day-to-day supply chain management.

Getting started with lean and sustaining it with continuous improvement is not easy. Lean takes time and years, to accomplish. There is no quick fix to being lean. Often the waste has become incorporated into the daily operation company-wide and is accepted as part of doing business. In some instances, there may be too much instability in a supply chain to begin lean. The first step is then to increase stability before beginning lean.

But the benefits can be significant from gaining market share, reducing capital tied up in inventory, increasing profitability, improving customer service, increasing capacity and taking time out of the entire company's way of doing things.

Chapter 31: Lean as a Supply Chain Strategy

Lean primarily refers to elimination of waste and is the basic philosophy that originated as part of Toyota Production Systems, with its emphasis on the elimination of waste (muda). Therefore, this philosophy is based on reducing the cost by eliminating activities that do not directly add any value. Cost can be reduced in two ways:

1. By identifying and eliminating the wasteful activities that don't add any value.
2. By enhancing the efficiency of a required activity so that the throughput of the process can be increased.

A lot of supply chain activities can directly leverage this thinking. Most execution activities in a supply chain can benefit from lean thinking, such as picking, packing, loading, and unloading in a warehouse; routing of shipments in transportation; labour activities on receiving docks at warehouses, stores, and manufacturing plants; and so on.

What does a lean design for a supply chain mean?

A lean supply chain design requires that supply chains minimize the cost of operations at all levels. Lean requires that the supply chain uses the least amount of resources to efficiently complete its job. The primary resources in a supply chain are inventory, warehouses, trucks, people, and working capital. A lean supply chain will be designed to have minimal inventories in the system, minimal amount of warehousing space required to store these inventories, and optimized shipments to reduce the cost of moving inventory. A lean supply chain will also be designed to establish long-term, stable supply contracts with the lowest negotiated cost, but typically without any substantial ability to change ordered quantities, delivery destinations, and required need dates after the order has been placed. Lean design will most likely not engage secondary suppliers, because a second tier of suppliers is expensive to maintain. All of these factors will reduce the costs of the supply chain operations, making it extremely cost-efficient, but will also constrain the supply chain's ability to adapt to any changes in demand, supply, or other resources, due to the built-in rigidity of the design.

And therein, lies the rub: Low inventories make the supply chain vulnerable to not being able to fulfil orders if the demand suddenly spikes or if there are changes in demand that were not foreseen. Inability to change orders with the suppliers also constrains the supply chain's ability to react to any changes in demand and may saddle the supply chain with unwanted inventory. Having no secondary suppliers also limits the ability of the supply chain to reacting to spikes in demand and/or exposes it to supply failures from the primary suppliers. The focus on being lean prevents this supply chain from building redundancy by design which reduces supply chain's ability to manage variability.

On the other hand, the only reason for supply chains to exist is to manage variability! So a lean focus in supply chain design actually goes against the very basic nature of the supply chains. However, if the lean focus is seen simply as the most efficient way to execute business operations (which include a fair amount of agility to respond to natural volatility in demand), then it can be used to design effective supply chains. Also if lean is a supply chain strategy that is good in certain conditions, I would like to know when is lean not good? When should a firm spend more money than is absolutely required to organize its operations?

Also, most firms have a large assortment of material to be managed: Raw materials, WIP, finished goods, and retail assortments almost always consist of a mixed bag of products when it comes to their demand profile. While some products may have a stable demand profile, others will be more volatile to manage. This means that the enterprise supply chain that must be designed to cater to all these types of products must be lean (to best manage the products with a stable demand) and agile (to manage others with volatile demand) simultaneously. After all, you could not run a business with a lean supply chain with the lowest cost, but that cannot respond to any changes in demand or supply. Since all demand and supply has inherent variability, such a rigidly designed supply chain will quickly build up unwanted and obsolete inventories as it is incapable of reacting to changes in demand and supply. Of course, too much emphasis on creating agility may be expensive and may also not provide the best design as we shall see when we discuss agile as a supply chain strategy.

Finally, the cost focus serves much better a generic business strategy as suggested by Michael Porter because a cost focus can be used effectively to drive any corporate function, such as accounting, human resources, merchandising, production planning, engineering and so on. There is nothing specific about the cost focus that would make it work any extra magic for supply chain than what it can do for any other corporate function, and hence its inability to drive supply chain strategy!

Chapter 32: Cost of Sales and Lean Supply Chain Competence

Supply chain competence affects your bottom-line in more direct ways than you might realize.

The cost of sales appears on the income statement right below the revenues. The difference between the revenues and the cost of sales is the gross profit. Therefore, the cost of sales directly determines the gross profit of a firm and that is directly responsible for the firm's bottom-line. It has several aliases; it may be called cost of goods sold, cost of products, cost of products sold or something else similar in connotation. That is not important. What is important is what constitutes the cost of sales. Typically, for manufacturers and retailers, it is also the second biggest number on the income statement after the revenues. In fact, for the financial year 2009, the COGS was 50% of 2009 revenues for P&G, 76% of the total revenues for Wal-Mart, and 70% of sales at Target for FY2009. Therefore, if one had to start looking at reducing costs, COGS fits the bill nicely. This is the largest pie of expense in an organization and even a small reduction in this will naturally generate a large impact on the firm's bottom-line.

What does cost of sales consist of?

Cost of sales generally includes all direct expenses related to the products or services that a firm sells. For manufacturers, this typically includes the cost of raw materials and purchased sub-assemblies, cost of conversion to the finished goods like the direct labour used to run a plant, depreciation of the plant and machinery, or things like the coolant oil needed to cut metal on the turning centres, cost of freight to transport raw-materials to its factories, warehousing costs to maintain the finished-goods stocks and shipping costs to ship them to their customers. In a retail scenario, the cost of sales will include the cost of merchandise and the cost of freight from its suppliers to its warehouses, and the cost of distribution from its warehouses to its stores. In summary; include all direct expenses related to the value-adding activities of the firm in the cost of sales.

So how can supply chain competency affect the cost of sales?

Almost all expenses related to the value-adding activities are controlled through the supply chain processes and the efficacy of these processes determines the cost basis of the activity. Take the warehousing costs, for example, automating the warehouse planning and execution activities through a warehouse management and execution system can increase the number of cases handled on inbound and outbound shipments for every labour-hour employed. The freight costs can be reduced by employing a better process for planning shipments that can reduce the miles driven, enhance the equipment utilization rates, or consolidate shipments to reduce freight. Any way you look at it, developing supply chain process competencies affects the process efficiencies that in turn, affect the cost of sales and hence your profitability.

Following are some of most common expenses included in the COGS and the supply chain process that can potentially optimize it.

Cost Component of COGS

Financial Metrics Affected
1. Direct Materials and Supplies, Cost of Raw Materials and Inputs (for manufacturers), or Merchandise (for retailers), etc.

2. Forecasting, Replenishment, Inventory Management (raw materials), Sourcing, Purchasing.

3. Gross Margin, EBITDA, Inventory, Inventory Turnover, Current Assets, Working Capital, Return on Assets.

4. Direct Labour, Cost of Transformation (production, manufacturing, processing, etc.), Depreciation, Direct Manufacturing Overheads, etc.

5. Production Planning, Factory Planning, Resource Planning, Inventory (work-in-progress) Management.

6. Gross Margin, EBITDA, Working Capital, Return on Capital Employed.

7. Cost of Freight (all inbound, outbound, and intra-facility transfers of material).

8. Transportation Management.

9. Cost of Warehousing, Inventory Shrink, Obsolescence, Mark-downs, Handling, Inventory Carrying.

10. Warehouse Management, Labour Management, Inventory Management (finished goods or merchandise).

The supply chain capabilities that can help reduce cost of sales are as follows.

1. The cost of materials, whether raw materials or merchandise, can be reduced through lean strategic sourcing, bid optimization, and supplier contracts-based optimization. Good demand and supply management practices also help in reducing the cost of materials by reducing obsolescence. Obsolete inventory typically results in merchandise clearance and write-offs both of which increase the total costs of materials.

2. Distribution costs primarily consist of warehousing and transportation. Supply chain processes that can help reduce these costs are lean distribution, lean network planning, lean warehouse management, and lean transportation management. The warehousing management capabilities reduce the warehousing costs through better use of

space, better inventory management in the warehouse, automation, and optimized labour scheduling. Network planning can reduce the cost of distribution through optimal positioning of the distribution centres with respect to the suppliers and stores. Transportation management capabilities help reduce the distribution costs by optimizing shipments that reduce the total miles driven and enhance the container and trailer volume utilization. Better fleet management capabilities can increase the efficiency of the fleet and freight invoice automation can reduce the expenses related to validating and paying for freight.

3. Manufacturing costs can be reduced through lean scheduling and factory planning processes. Supply chain optimization solutions that allow modelling of the demand, available inventory, available resources, operations, and sequencing constraints are typically used to produce feasible manufacturing schedules that can optimize the usage of assets and resources to produce manufacturing schedules that drive most profitable product-mix for the given demand or maximize the demand fulfilment for given orders. Increasing the asset utilization reduces need for investing in capital assets thus reducing long-term debt used to finance capital investments. In turn, it positively impacts return on capital employed by reducing the total current liabilities.

4. Major labour costs for the retailers occur in the warehouses and the stores, and for manufacturers, they are in the factories. Lean warehouse management processes can help directly reduce the labour costs in the warehouses, by better labour planning, scheduling, and task tracking. Better demand forecasting in the stores helps in streamlining the labour plans in the stores. Manufacturing labour costs are minimized through lean scheduling and factory planning capabilities that can model the material and asset constraints to produce feasible labour plans.

Any reduction in the cost of sales directly translates into increased margins assuming the other factors remain constant.

Chapter 33: Putting Lean into Supply Chain

The What, the Why and the How of Supply Chains

Like anything else, understanding what a supply chain is important. This field of management has been evolving. What was considered supply chain management a decade ago has emerged, evolved, and extended. As firms realize how integrated their operations really are, the scope of functions considered as part of the supply chain processes continues to extend. Supply chains have been around since the industrial revolution began mass-production in early 1900s, but they have never been studied, developed, and managed with so much thought and consideration. For all these reasons, then, it is important to understand the what of supply chains.

But that is a start, not an end in itself.

Once you understand what supply chains are, the why and the how start. After all, there is no problem that can be solved without understanding the why and the how. That is where the lean supply chain management comes in. This is a process that provides a functional tour of the supply chain processes in a firm. Instead of dwelling on the what, it dwells on the why and the how. Lean supply chain management is a simple and straightforward process that provide an overview of the supply chain functions in an enterprise; and, for each, provide a brief why (why is this function important, what questions does it answer?), and a brief how (how does the function address the questions, what are the process inputs and outputs).

As we know that Supply chain management (SCM) is management of a network of interconnected businesses involved in the provision of product and service packages required by the end customers in a supply chain; supply chain management spans all movement and storage of raw materials, work-in-process inventory, and finished goods from point of origin to point of consumption.

Lean supply chain manage upstream and down-stream value added flow of materials, final goods and related information among suppliers; company; resellers; final consumers is supply chain management.

Lean supply chain management is the systematic, strategic coordination of the traditional business functions and the tactics across these business functions within a particular company and across businesses within the supply chain, for the purposes of improving the long-term performance of the individual companies and the supply chain as a whole.

We must remember that lean supply chain strategies require a total systems view of the linkages in the chain that work together efficiently to create customer satisfaction at the end point of delivery to the consumer. As a consequence costs must be lowered throughout the chain by driving out unnecessary costs and focusing attention on adding value. Throughput efficiency must be increased, bottlenecks removed and performance measurement must focus on total systems efficiency and equitable reward distribution to those in the supply chain adding value. The lean supply chain system must be responsive to customer requirements therefore lean supply chain management is the integration of key business processes across the supply chain for the purpose of creating value for customers and stakeholders.

Chapter 34: Problems Addressed by Lean Supply Chain Management

Supply chain management encompasses the planning and management of all activities involved in sourcing, procurement, conversion, and logistics management. It also includes the crucial components of coordination and collaboration with channel partners, which can be suppliers, intermediaries, third-party service providers, and customers. In essence, supply chain management integrates supply and demand management within and across companies. More recently, the loosely coupled, self-organizing network of businesses that cooperate to provide product and service offerings has been called the Extended Enterprise.

A supply chain, as opposed to supply chain management, is a set of organizations directly linked by one or more of the upstream and downstream flows of products, services, finances, and information from a source to a customer.

In many cases the supply chain includes the collection of goods after consumer use for recycling. Including 3PL or other gathering agencies as part of the RM repatriation process is a way of illustrating the new endgame strategy.

Lean supply chain management must address the following problems:

1. **Distribution Network Configuration:** number, location and network missions of suppliers, production facilities, distribution centres, warehouses, cross-docks and customers.

2. **Distribution Strategy:** questions of operating control (centralized, decentralized or shared); delivery scheme, e.g., direct shipment, pool point shipping, cross docking, direct store delivery (DSD), closed loop shipping; mode of transportation, e.g., motor carrier, including truckload, Less than truckload (LTL), parcel; railroad; intermodal transport, including trailer on flatcar (TOFC) and container on flatcar (COFC); ocean freight; airfreight; replenishment strategy (e.g., pull, push or hybrid); and transportation control (e.g., owner-operated, private carrier, common carrier, contract carrier, or third-party logistics (3PL)).

3. **Trade-Offs in Logistical Activities:** The above activities must be well coordinated in order to achieve the lowest total logistics cost. Trade-offs may increase the total cost if only one of the activities is optimized. For example, full truckload (FTL) rates are more economical on a cost per pallet basis than LTL shipments. If, however, a full truckload of a product is ordered to reduce

transportation costs, there will be an increase in inventory holding costs which may increase total logistics costs. It is therefore imperative to take a systems approach when planning logistical activities. These trade-offs are key to developing the most efficient and effective Logistics and SCM strategy.

4. **Information:** Integration of processes through the supply chain to share valuable information, including demand signals, forecasts, inventory, transportation, potential collaboration, etc.

5. **Inventory Management:** Quantity and location of inventory, including raw materials, work-in-process (WIP) and finished goods.

6. **Cash-Flow:** Arranging the payment terms and methodologies for exchanging funds across entities within the supply chain.

Lean supply chain execution means managing and coordinating the movement of materials, information and funds across the supply chain. The flow is bi-directional.

Chapter 35: Lean Supply Chain as a Cross-function

Lean supply chain management is a cross-function approach including managing the movement of raw materials into an organization, certain aspects of the internal processing of materials into finished goods, and the movement of finished goods out of the organization and toward the end-consumer.

As organizations strive to focus on core competencies and becoming more flexible, they reduce their ownership of raw materials sources and distribution channels. These functions are increasingly being outsourced to other entities that can perform the activities better or more cost effectively. The effect is to increase the number of organizations involved in satisfying customer demand, while reducing management control of daily logistics operations.

Less control and more supply chain partners led to the creation of supply chain management concepts. The purpose of supply chain management is to improve trust and collaboration among supply chain partners, thus improving inventory visibility and the velocity of inventory movement.

Organizations increasingly find that they must rely on effective supply chains, or networks, to compete in the global market and networked economy. In Peter Drucker's (1998) new management paradigms, this concept of business relationships extends beyond traditional enterprise boundaries and seeks to organize entire business processes throughout a value chain of multiple companies.

During the past decades, globalization, outsourcing and information technology have enabled many organizations, such as Dell and Apple, to successfully operate solid collaborative supply networks in which each specialized business partner focuses on only a few key strategic activities. This inter-organizational supply network can be acknowledged as a new form of organization. However, with the complicated interactions among the players, the network structure fits neither "market" nor "hierarchy" categories. It is not clear what kind of performance impacts different supply network structures could have on firms, and little is known about the coordination conditions and trade-offs that may exist among the players. From a systems perspective, a complex network structure can be decomposed into individual component firms.

Traditionally, companies in a supply network concentrate on the inputs and outputs of the processes, with little concern for the internal management working of other individual players. Therefore, the choice of an internal management control structure is known to impact local firm performance.

In the 21st century, changes in the business environment have contributed to the development of lean supply chain networks. First, as an outcome of globalization and the proliferation of multinational companies, joint ventures, strategic alliances and business partnerships, significant success factors were identified, complementing the earlier "Just-In-Time", Lean Manufacturing and Agile manufacturing practices. Second, technological changes, particularly the dramatic fall in information communication costs, which are a significant component of transaction costs, have led to changes in coordination among the members of the supply chain network

Many researchers have recognized these kinds of supply network structures as a new organization form, using terms such as "Keiretsu", "Extended Enterprise", "Virtual Corporation", "Global Production Network", and "Next Generation Manufacturing System". In general, such a structure can be defined as "a group of semi-independent organizations, each with their capabilities, which collaborate in ever-changing constellations to serve one or more markets in order to achieve some business goal specific to that collaboration.

Chapter 36: Lean Supply Chain Management Transformation

Lean supply chain management transformation is a strategic imperative for any manufacturer. This new perspective is one that will continue to gain importance, sees all suppliers and customers as part of one complex supply chain network and understands that transforming that supply chain into a synchronized chain is the primary goal.

Lean supply chain management transformation provides fast access to relevant and accurate information. This timely supply chain information can pay off handsomely in lower costs, less inventory, improved throughput, shorter cycle times, and the highest levels of customer service. The very essence of supply chain management is effective information and material flow throughout a network of customers and suppliers. By using the Internet, companies simply have better and more far-reaching ways to speed up the information flow process and make it more effective.

For many companies, it is now clear that the supply chain that best manages the flows of both information and material can significantly differentiate itself from its competitors. As customers and suppliers band together in mutually beneficial partnerships, the need for better and better supply chain management processes and systems becomes more critical. Within the boardroom, improving supply chain management is getting lots of attention because forward-thinking management teams know it is the best strategy to increase and maintain market share while at the same time increasing profits. Experts now agree that in many industries, market share will be won and lost based on supply chain performance.

Good supply chain practitioners know that information should be passed on only to those who need to know it, when they need to know it, and in the form they need to have it in. Changes in demand information, inventory positions, order fulfilment, supply management, and a whole host of other information exchange activities will transform how we sell products, supply products, and make and receive payments for goods and services. Tomorrow's supply chain will link customers and suppliers together seamlessly throughout the world. The higher speed of information flow itself will in turn mandate faster flows of material, which only lean manufacturing operations can generate.

Executive management is taking a good hard look at supply chains and finding a dysfunctional mix of processes, policies, systems, communications, performance measures, and organizational accountability. Some of these processes are clearly functionally divided silos; those barricaded "power pockets" of the internally focused corporate hierarchical maze that was the standard for decades. Other processes are hybrid and include everything from manual order entry to faxes and phone communications and e-mail. Still other processes reveal the current trend toward full electronic communication and collaboration throughout the supply chain, including automated order entry, delivery tracking, and inventory planning systems. Whatever the exact mix, it is clear that most companies have a long way to go before they will have fully transformed their supply chain for the twenty-first century.

Chapter 37: Lean E-Supply Chain Management

Two very compelling reasons justify pursuing lean e-supply chain management. First, suppliers are now integrating, rather than just interfacing, with their customers.

There's no small difference between interfacing and integrating. Whereas interfacing indicates communication through some means or other, integrating indicates a more far-reaching connection through electronic business processes. Before, a company might send a monthly report to suppliers about what orders they expect to come in that month, now it is feasible to let suppliers check your order status at any and every point during the month, including in real time. In an integrated supply chain, customers and suppliers become mutually dependent by collaborating through the shared goal of the streamlined, efficient demand and supply process. The objective is for everyone in the supply chain to increase market share through quick responses to customer needs. This can only happen when information, materials, and products flow smoothly and freely, in sync with demand. It's a formidable task but the effort can pay big dividends, including making (or breaking) marketplace leadership.

The second reason to pursue the lean e-supply chain is related but different in emphasis. While the first reason emphasizes filling customers' product needs, the second emphasizes improving the performance of manufacturing material flow and all the benefits those improvements can bring. Many companies now recognize that flow through the entire supply chain is the critical factor for success. In fact, in the future, customers will want to work only with suppliers who are consistently flexible and responsive in meeting their supply needs. The objectives for improved supply chain management are twofold, affecting both the cost and revenue sides of the business equation. The goals are:

1. Gain a competitive advantage and increase market share by being more flexible, quicker, more dependable, and less costly.

2. Achieve better cost efficiency through high-speed information and material flows with lower inventories and decreased overhead activity costs.

Like manufacturing processes, supply chain processes involve the flow of information and materials. The information flow precedes and causes material to continue (or stop) flowing through the supply chain. Thus, your supply chain material flow will, by and large, only be as good as the information that drives it.

Chapter 38: The Goal of the Lean Supply Chain

A lean supply chain defines how a well-designed supply chain should operate, delivering products quickly to the end customer, with minimum waste. A lean supply chain is a great enabler for any organization that strives to become more lean and efficient.

Organizations within a lean supply chain are able to leverage their own lean journey more easily, delivering better customer value by responding more efficiently, quickly, and predictably to customer needs. That, in turn, facilitates the operation of the lean supply chain, creating a virtuous cycle that ultimately translates to superior financial performance for these organizations.

Thus organizations striving to become lean would benefit from a systematic approach towards building and managing their supply chain. A recent study that analyzed the link between supply chain and financial performance revealed that virtually all winning business strategies have, at their core, supply chain strategies that provide a competitive advantage.

Seven Steps for Building Lean Supply Chains

These steps are:
1. Develop Systems Thinking
2. Understand Customer Value

3. Value Stream Mapping
4. Benchmark Best Practices
5. Design to Manage Demand Volatility
6. Create Flow
7. Performance Metrics

These seven steps have been recently applied by several organizations in their lean journey, to increase their competitive advantage and profitability, while at the same time enabling their supply chain partners become more efficient and productive.

Develop a Systems Perspective

A vital first step is to develop a systems perspective. The systems perspective recognizes that if each element in the supply chain tries to optimize its own operations in isolation, everyone suffers in the long run. For instance, supply chain management requires long-term partnerships with key suppliers.

Suppose management institutes a measurement system that rewards the Purchase department for obtaining products from its suppliers at low cost. No doubt, reduced material costs directly affect the profitability of the organization, but such a measurement system drives the Purchase department into an adversarial position with its suppliers, encouraging Purchase to play off potential suppliers against each other in an attempt to drive them to lower their prices. The lack of a systems perspective has now made it very difficult to establish long-term partnerships with the organization's suppliers. The Theory of Constraints (TOC) avoids the pitfalls of such local thinking by adopting a global perspective, with the objective of maximizing the organization's profit. Application of TOC principles provides a number of levers for systems thinking and supply chain coordination.

Map the Value Stream

The value stream map illustrates the structure of the physical flow of goods and information flow, and highlights areas in the value stream (supply chain) that require more attention. A comprehensive map will highlights weak links in the value stream, identifying opportunities for removing muda, mura, or muri, three Japanese words that respectively mean wastefulness, unevenness and overburdening. Muda exists in the form of unnecessary, non-value added. Mura exists in a variety of forms; unevenness in quality, unevenness in sales and production, or unevenness in supplier delivery performance. Muri can be the result of, for instance, unevenness in the demand, that could overburden some of the resources, albeit temporarily. It could also exist due to the presence of either physical constraints or some policies that create artificial constraints.

Design Products and Processes to Manage Demand Volatility

One of the barriers to an organization's quest to become lean is that the customer demand is unpredictable, and therefore the organization is forced to carry some finished goods inventory, resulting in a supply chain that is no longer lean.

171

However, better understanding on why customer demand is volatile can pay huge dividends, because typically the end-customer demand is flat, or has very little variation, and much of the demand volatility experienced by organizations in the supply chain is due to the well-known bullwhip effect. And having more inventory at each intermediate stage in the supply chain to buffer against uncertainty is usually not the right answer because it actually makes the supply chain more sluggish in responding to changes in end-customer demand. If the end-customer sees a long delay in response to orders, he/she is likely to pad his/her real demand by a safety factor, to hedge against uncertain lead times, leading to more inventory and more uncertainty in the system. We thus observe that quite often, demand volatility can be self-induced! On the flip side, if you respond quickly to demands, customers will have more faith in your ability to deliver and are therefore less likely to pad their actual requirements or their desired due dates.

Another example of self-induced volatility is due to batching. While the end-user demand for a product may be fairly level, organizations often deliver products in large lots to achieve scale economies, again resulting in a bullwhip effect. The obvious solution is to produce in small lots, to the extent possible.

A very useful approach to manage demand volatility, especially when designing supply chains that deal with high product variety and demand volatility, is to "maximize external variety with minimal internal variety." This principle can be accomplished by structuring product offerings so that commitment of material and resources is postponed for as long as possible. In other words, the idea is to work with a relatively small number of standard products ("modules") in semi-finished or finished form to configure a large variety of end products.

Develop Metrics Using a Systems Perspective

The performance of a supply chain is the result of policies and procedures that drive various critical segments of the supply chain. The question is, "How can we design metrics to manage organizations recognizing that these organizations are components of complex and highly interconnected systems?"

This question is rapidly gaining importance as supply chain managers face increased pressures on customer service and asset performance. Sony, for instance, is acutely aware of the fact that any inventory of its products at Best Buy and Circuit City ultimately affects its profitability if it remains on the shelf for more than a few days. Sony has changed its delivery metric from "sell-in" to "sell-through." The difference is that the former metric allowed its Sales department to chalk up a sale when the product was shipped to the customer (Best Buy, Circuit City, etc.) whereas the latter metric chalks up a sale only when the product is sold and paid for. To give another example, Procter & Gamble uses its VMI process to routinely measure both its own inventory and the downstream inventory of its products.

As a useful guideline, when developing metrics, it is worth asking whether a metric under consideration.

1. Helps sell more products, profitably,
2. Helps reduce investments in resources or,
3. Helps reduce payments or expenses over the long term.

If the answer to all these questions is no, then that metric must be questioned.

Chapter 39: Ways to Get a Lean Supply Chain

Moving towards a lean supply chain means eliminating waste in three ways:

1. Reducing working capital.
2. Enhancing operational productivity.
3. Improving "build-in" quality and reliability (implementing quality controls on the front end of any process or procedure).

Here are 10 ways to get lean Supply Chain

1. Make your supply chain more compact. Optimize the flow of goods and information through the supply chain. Implement plant and warehouse layouts and designs that streamline inbound and outbound flows.

2. Reduce stock at point-of-use. To support a flexible production schedule, keep a variety of part numbers on hand in the warehouse. By executing lean logistics techniques such as sequencing and sub-assembly you can avoid large inventory stocks and their associated costs.

3. Balance the receipt and delivery of goods. Matching the incoming and outgoing flow of material to customer demands minimizes the amount of material stored in the supply chain, resulting in lower costs.

4. Reduce capital expenditures by closely managing your empty container flow. The reverse logistics process of handling empty containers can be complex, so it needs to be well-managed to guarantee reliable supply and the lowest level of damage. At the same time, a well-managed empty container flow can significantly reduce maintenance and container replacement costs.

5. Balance the work so your cycle time hits close to Takt Time. Every task performed by an operator needs to fall close to Takt Time; the pace of production in each process that is necessary to satisfy customer demand. This scheduling will help ensure minimal waiting time and maximum productivity.

6. Optimize transportation routes. Employ recognized transportation best practices to improve the efficiency of moving goods off the production line and into delivery. By applying concepts such as segregating flows into small and large lots, direct dock-to-line feeding, and combining cycles (one full against one empty), you can avoid wasteful internal transportation processes and optimize available resources.

7. Optimize delivery. Avoid unnecessary replenishment through the use of Kanban and other pull systems. These systems result in replenishment based on consumption, keeping inventory lean.

8. Standardize warehouse processes. Implement stable and repeatable processes, and standardize the time it takes to perform tasks such as picking, packing, and put away. Standardization helps the warehouse interface more accurately and efficiently with operations outside the four walls, such as transportation.

9. Use visual management aids for information flow. Visual aids are an important part of tracking the physical flow of materials in a plant or warehouse. If everyone on the shop floor can "see" the current production status, they can more easily react to peaks and valleys.

10. End and correct line stoppages. Stopping the production line is costly and often unnecessary. When a problem arises, don't let it go and plan to fix it later. Stop and correct the problem now. You might temporarily slow productivity, but in the long run recurring problems should end

Chapter 40: Value Stream and Lean

Value stream mapping is one of the key elements of Lean and Lean Six Supply Chain methodologies. Without adequate information about the value stream for a specific business operation, implementing improvements and increasing efficiency would be less than optimal at best.

But what exactly is the value stream and why is it such an important concept within the Lean philosophy?

The value stream for a business process is the series of steps that occur to provide the product, service and/or experience the customer desires. Steps that do not add value, that represent waste or that a customer does not want and would not pay for are not part of the value stream.

Customer Value

Business leaders often have trouble distinguishing between steps that for technical or business reasons must be included and steps that are actually value-added (VA) according to the customer expectations. A good question to ask is, if this step was deleted would the customer complain? If the answer is yes, the step is truly VA; if not, it cannot be considered VA, no matter how necessary it is for the business to provide the final product or service. Other questions to ask are whether the customer would pay more for the product or service or have a preference for it over the competition with that task included.

Identifying the Value Stream

In identifying the value stream for a business process, it is helpful to evaluate each step based on the criteria above to assess whether it is value-added (VA) or non-value added (NVA). To do this, solid information about customer expectations for quality and value must be obtained; assumptions about what customers want and expect are not sufficient. Some groups find it useful to add a third category to represent steps that are not VA, but that really must be conducted to create the final product or service. These steps are referred to as business-value added (BVA) steps and may include tasks required by regulatory bodies or for company financial reporting.

Objectives

Once the value stream is identified, the ultimate goal is to eliminate all other steps from the process. Steps that are NVA should definitely be removed; BVA steps should be re-evaluated and eliminated if possible. By making these improvements, an organization can improve efficiency, reduce waste and improve the customer experience.

Continuous Improvement

It may be tempting to think about identifying the value stream and eliminating NVA steps as a one-time project. However, customer needs and expectations can change over time, so existing products and services should be assessed periodically to ensure the originally identified value stream still applies and is being followed. The value stream should also be clarified prior to establishing new products and services.

Chapter 41: Internet Enabled Lean Supply Chain

Lean SCM is a supply chain operational and strategic management philosophy that utilizes Internet-enabling technologies to effect the continuous regeneration of supplier and service partner networks. A lean supply chain network is empowered to execute superlative, unique customer-winning value at the lowest cost through the collaborative, real-time synchronization of product/service transfer, demand priorities, vital marketplace information and logistics delivery capabilities.

The critical components of this definition are revealing. To begin with, Internet enabled supply chain operational and strategic management philosophy defines the scope of lean SCM. The continuous regeneration of networks of supply channel partners concept implies that companies succeed in the 21st century by generating constantly evolving networks of supply chain partners. Such continuously evolving networks can respond to the dynamic nature of today's ongoing demand for new forms of customer/supplier collaboration and scalable product and information delivery flows. Today's companies compete by the quality of their supply chains.

Unique customer-winning value refers to the ability of companies to assemble agile, scalable production/distribution systems capable of continuously reinventing unique product and service configurations and value-creating relationships. This element defines the mission of all trading partners. And finally, collaborative, real-time synchronization refers to the application of technology process enablers that network internal enterprise systems, decision support tools and data warehouses to merge, optimize and effectively direct supply chain competencies. This element describes the mechanics of how Internet-enabled supply chains compete.

Lean supply chain management is grounded in these principles, but focuses on the most effective management of supply chain ecosystems. In today's extremely competitive environment, global sourcing has vastly expanded the number of potential players.

Consequently excellent logistics execution is more important than ever; supply chain ecosystems must quickly eliminate nodes that are unproductive. At the same time, they must stabilize themselves by ensuring that proven partners survive and prosper.

To succeed and lead, the entire supply chain ecosystem must continuously adapt and adopt the following six mechanisms:
1. e-Information: Information accumulated, tracked, monitored and harnessed over the Internet.
2. Supply chain synchronization.
3. Supply chain collaboration.
4. Optimization.
5. Operations excellence.
6. Connectivity and networking.

We will review all of the above six mechanisms in the next few chapters.

Chapter 42: Lean e-Information

If the prime driver of SCM is information, then the faster information can be gathered, analyzed and diffused through the channel network, the more competitive supply chain trading partners will be. Internet technology provides the means to make real-time demand management, manufacturing, logistics and storage data visible to all trading partners. Internet-enabled data enables trading partners to integrate supply chain interactive processes such as vendor-managed inventory.

These trading-partner transactions can be broken down into five areas:

1. Customer e-intelligence

Lean SCM's first challenge is to understand and respond effectively to customer needs and requirements. Partners need to:

    a. Gather and share demand management intelligence regarding the validity of forecasts, the impact of out-of-bounds events, and actual product/service mix usage occurring at any point in the channel. All too often companies are planning based on the demand generated by orders for delivery to stores. Weeks later they find that some styles have not been selling and have to be marked down and others sold out early in the season. Getting timely information about actual consumer sales electronically from the point-of-sale systems enables companies to truly move towards a demand-driven environment.

b. Unearth data regarding the impact of pricing and promotion decisions governing channel fulfilment. Tools in this area need to provide intelligence as to the velocity of sales and the timely reporting of revenues, costs and profits.

c. Detail the status of channel inventories, optimize the trade-off between capacity utilization and customer service, and enable replenishment visibility and rapid redeployment of channel inventories.

2. Logistics e-information

Demand intelligence linked with logistics data can determine the optimal use of transportation and warehouse resources to maximize customer fulfilment value. Supply chain partners need visibility on internal and external logistics functions so that they can allocate resources to best meet a specific demand flow.

Logistics planners likewise need accessible real-time intelligence in order to configure unique value networks. To be successful, planners will require Web-based applications that enable cross-channel system interoperability to provide insight into the status and velocity of production capacities, storage capabilities, inventory availability and replenishment processes, and transportation resources at each node in the supply network.

Channel network resource alignment e-information. Cost-efficient SCM requires timely intelligence as to the positioning and planned allocation of products and services as they exist in the network at any given time. The optimal allocation of demand-satisfying resources requires knowing the total cost of customer service throughout the demand chain. Tools such as activity-based costing, the balanced scorecard, or the supply chain operations reference model (SCOR) graphically identify pools of costs residing at the points where trading partner processes intersect.

These tools/models must be capable of determining such critical fulfilment values as reliability, responsiveness, flexibility, cost and efficiency of asset utilization, and be able to communicate the metrics in real-time to other channel constituents.

3. Product and process e-information

Companies have turned to the Internet for assistance in three major production-related areas.

    a. Web-based tool sets to execute product design content synchronization. Today's design teams are linked together by real-time concurrent peer-to-peer (P2P) technologies that create interoperable knowledge repositories linking CAE/CAM systems, product data management (PDM) systems, direct customer configuration feeds and design collaboration software (DCS).

b. Online trading communities that facilitate product and supplier search, order status and tracking, product catalogues, and buyer/supplier back-end integration.
c. The application of cross-channel advanced planning and scheduling (APS) systems.

4. e-Procurement information.

Working with suppliers today requires two types of information; intelligence about collaborative relationships and projects, and intelligence about supplier capabilities. Both are focused on a single objective to reduce supply chain risk. While many companies in the past attempted to utilize EDI or merge ERP output, the results were inward facing. They did little to further the integration and collaborative relationships necessary to enhance the speed of transfer and depth of information that sales and manufacturing management need.

Internet-based technologies are rapidly making this supplier intelligence gap disappear. Today's cutting-edge companies can assemble a complete picture of their supply relationships.

5. e-RFQs, auctions

e-RFQs are electronic requests for quotations; a type of mini electronic tender where the buyers can buy or source goods and services that are either not suitable for catalogue content or have a fluctuating price, often from pre-negotiated framework contracts.

Trading exchanges, logistics interfaces, automated shopping applications, and Web-enabled services such as strategic sourcing, fulfilment, collaborative design, and finance and billing.

Chapter 43: Lean Supply Chain Synchronization

The real challenge is to present real-time information concurrently so that all supply chain partners can receive and utilize it at the same time. The benefits are obvious.

Synchronization of demand/supply information minimizes work-in-process and finished goods inventories up and down the channel, dampens the "bullwhip effect" as products are pulled through the distribution pipeline, reduces costs overall, and matches customer requirements with available products.

To be of value, supply chain synchronization requires all members of the ecosystem to engage in partnerships that collectively optimize resources and reduce costs. A synchronized supply chain will consist of the following key components;
   a. A unified business strategy.
   b. Common measurements for product and performance excellence.
   c. The selection of enabling technologies.

Unified business strategy

No company today possesses all the strengths needed to remain competitive by itself. As such, the creation of business strategies rightfully extends beyond a company's boundaries and should be folded within an inter-channel effort. Such efforts result in the formulation of joint strategies that foster the use of optimal, cost-effective methods of designing, building and delivering unique, customer-winning value to the marketplace by leveraging the capabilities of the entire supply chain.

Common measurements

Effective supply chain synchronization requires that all trading partners collectively achieve operations excellence. This requires more effort than simply establishing electronic transactions or sharing forecasts. It requires synchronizing the performance of each channel member and blending the performance measurements into a total supply chain balanced scorecard. Expect the Supply Chain Council's Supply Chain Operations Reference (SCOR) to keep gaining popularity for this purpose. The SCOR model includes a cross-functional framework, standard terminology, common metrics and best practices that can be applied to entire supply chains.

Selection of enabling technologies

To synchronize the channel, trading partners must synchronize their internal business systems. Web-based applications are beginning to giving participating partners access to the applications and objectives of each supply network node. The goal for the future is development of interoperable process components that enable whole supply chains to access selected data from the databases and processes of member ERP backbones; front and back-end applications such as CRM, HTML/XML document integration, data warehouses and various trading exchanges.

Chapter 44: Lean Supply Chain Collaboration

Perhaps the most critical component of lean SCM is the willingness of channel members to engage in and constantly enhance collaborative relationships. Many companies have come to realize that short-term benefits brought about by logistics optimization and technology automation are incapable of producing the radical competitive breakthroughs that can be attained when channel partners strive to build long-term collaborative relationships.

As a supply network, the dominant characteristics of lean SCM are collaboration and synchronization. Collaboration is essentially the ability to share and interact upon critical data. Synchronization means possessing the channel intelligence to access the right product and the right service in the supply chain to satisfy the customer.

Lean SCM is not just about employing Internet-enabled information and synchronization tools. It demands that companies up and down the supply chain embrace the accompanying cultural and organizational changes as well.

Collaboration occurs in increasing intensity within both the technical and business spheres. Technical collaboration ramps up from fax to EDI, server-to-server links and Internet applications providing real-time information and transaction synchronization.

Business collaboration ramps up from a bare minimum to joint operations, coordination of network partner competencies and joint visioning where partners cooperate and compete as if they were a single channel entity.

Each level of collaboration generates value through four critical drivers:

1. The collaborative capacity of intra-company management teams grows in proportion to the level of collaboration intensity.
2. As collaborative intensity grows it drives exponential growth in more complex technical and business infrastructures to create and extract value.
3. While joint business processes within the channel are critical for creating collaborative value, they are just the start of many possibilities.
4. Strategic planners must constantly search for and implement new technologies and management methods.

While no one can disagree on the power of collaboration, there are many barriers that inhibit implementation. Corporate inertia and internal performance silos often pose an almost insurmountable barrier to building an environment that encourages openness, communication and mutual dependence.

Another barrier is lack of trust. Companies fear that proprietary information will be broadcast to partners who will in turn pass it on to competitors or use it to unfair advantage. The best collaborative relationships typically take years of good will, investment in resources and proof of mutual benefit.

In addition, collaboration has often been confused with process reengineering. While collaboration will increase efficiencies, such a short-term understanding misses the real advantages. They are found in the leveraging of channel competencies, utilization of cross-channel best practices and innovation.

Last but not least, the incompatibility of trading partners' system platforms poses a serious deterrent to shared communications.

Chapter 45: Lean Optimization, Operations Excellence, Connectivity and Networking

Lean Optimization

A supply chain ecosystem must be capable of utilizing process management and technology tools to continuously optimize productive resources. Optimization requires the pursuit and merger of three levels of improvement.

1. First is the lean principle discussed earlier in this book; a focus on eliminating waste and engineering "perfect" processes on the company level. It aims to reduce costs while at the same time providing for the establishment of new sources of customer value.

2. Second is the pursuit of optimization across trading partner relationships and systems. This initiative is much harder to accomplish. Channel nodes must closely collaborate, synchronize and integrate processes. The goal is to bring about value chain-wide processes that promote cost savings, efficiencies and productivities that make the entire supply chain ecosystem more competitive.

3. Finally, lean SCM optimization requires the standardization and rationalization of all supply channel processes. In detail, this effort

201

seeks to remove the impediments caused by batch and queue thinking within separate operations. In general, this principle assists partners in removing the same barriers in the supply chain and integrating the design, production and transfer of goods and information. It also helps ensure that customer-satisfying efforts are centred in the most efficient points in the supply network.

Operations Excellence

The foundation for effective lean SCM lies in the ability of entire supply chain networks to achieve superlative levels of collaborative operations excellence. The SCM standard of excellence requires trading partners to coordinate technology and processes in order to provide the highest level of customer fulfilment and service, while at the same time managing multiple levels of external relationships. Establishing both the framework and content of such a robust level of channel synchronization requires deep commitment, trust, and the willingness and capacity to acquire and expand new skills.

Is it worth it? Yes, because this effort provides real options, meaning opportunities to make decisions in the future based on the outcome of things that are uncertain today. Timely information gives companies in the supply chain real options to mitigate risks. For example, by having a real-time handle on demand pull, network trading partners can strategically plan and deploy safety stocks, determine the optimal point for product postponement, allocate capital, and minimize the impact of volume variances due to forecast error or demand fluctuations.

On the customer services side, real-time information enables companies to integrate customers directly into their business systems, thus increasing responsiveness, tracking order flow in real time and gathering channel-wide performance statistics. On the shop floor, real-time information improves planners' forward visibility into supplier capacities to smooth capacity spikes and improve throughput. In the supply channel, real-time information provides the bridge between company-level optimization planning and the global demand pull of the entire business network. In short, shared real-time information enables the generation of portfolio of triggerable decisions with options to proceed or abandon by milestone.

Connectivity and Networking

Connectivity and networking are lean supply chain fundamentals. Connectivity presupposes the availability of a technical infrastructure that links computer systems and people.
The word commonly used for this process is integration; a term often erroneously used as a synonym to connectivity and interfacing.

To clarify:
   1. Connectivity means connecting processes together, such as when a telephone system

connects customers and order processing functions.

2. Interfacing means bringing information from one system and presenting it for input to another, such as occurs in an EDI transaction.

3. Organizationally, integration means leveraging information tools that bring business functions together by facilitating ever-closer coordination in the execution of joint business processes.

The integration effort focuses on activating the creative thinking within and between enterprises. It attempts to align the challenges and opportunities offered by information technologies and the cultures and capabilities of the modern organization.

The second fundamental technology dimension is networking; connecting different computers and their databases together in a peer-to-peer network. Targeted at solving the problem of dissimilar hardware operating systems, networked systems enable people to communicate directly both within the enterprise and across the entire value chain. Connectivity is the process of linking business functions together; networking activates those links.

Chapter 46: Mastering Lean vs. Employee Resistance

The single biggest roadblock to successful implementation of Lean is employee acceptance. Yet most companies fail to address the problems created by the cultural change that going Lean requires. Typically firms introduce Lean by training a few "black belts" who then train the trainers in a sort of "trickle down" approach. But for most workers, Lean training focuses on how to do the job, not why they need to do it differently. What is lacking is enterprise-wide motivational training.

A client of ours has experienced the benefits that motivational exercises can bring to a Lean strategy. A UK based manufacturer was transformed from a hierarchal management style into one consisting of self-supervised teams. In the process the company has become a world leader in its field of business.

Prior to going Lean, the company was suffering from engineering delays, product log jams, inventory control issues, materials handling problems, clutter and numerous other related difficulties. The inefficiencies were not limited to the manufacturing side, either. Sales and marketing, engineering and executive offices have all since been reorganized and transformed.

Today the company employs Lean cellular work areas throughout the organization including office layouts which has led to better organization and easier access to equipment. By going Lean, the company has realized a 60% increase in throughput over the old paradigm. Sales are up 10% and profits up 120%.

Simulations Deliver High Psychological Impact

The most difficult aspect of going Lean was in structuring the company's now-standard self-supervised teams. To help differentiate the new self-supervised teams structure it was striving for from the old hierarchical style it wanted to change, we put everyone in the company through an exercise called Lean Manufacturing. Management held discussions before and after each simulation to reinforce the fact that this was a proven organizational model.

In the simulation, participants use interlocking plastic blocks to produce model cars. During phase one; participants build their cars using a traditional plant layout. In phases two and three, they redesign their work area into a cellular layout and learn to utilize one-piece workflow with a pull system. In the final phase, they experience the concepts of a flexible workforce and load levelling.

To gain improvement in its marketing, sales and administration functions we used Lean Office. This program puts nine participants to work in a fictional company where they learn to improve the quotation process.

We found that the motivational exercises had a tremendous psychological impact on employees. By providing a visual contrast of the old work processes and the new procedures, the exercises clearly demonstrated the benefits of change. Furthermore, employees quickly grasped an understanding of the individual roles they would play in the new organization.

The company experience demonstrates the inestimable value of winning over employees by involving them in the continuous improvement process toward a fully-realized Lean environment. The company learned that individuals were capable of contributing far more than the company's original management system allowed, and that the team's concept could provide the company with a competitive advantage.

Managing Change

Employee motivation is certainly not the only challenge to Lean adoption; however, companies that want to achieve higher returns on their improvement programs need to incorporate such change management techniques into their adoption strategies, along with a plan for basic education of all employees in Lean fundamentals.

Studies show that the more aggressively companies adopt Lean strategies, the more success they enjoy. Companies that have mastered Lean basics are meeting or exceeding shareholder expectations. According to our research, approximately 80% of best-in-class, 60% of industry average, and 40% of laggard companies are meeting, if not exceeding, expectations in key areas such as the reduction of inventory and assets, manufacturing and design cost reductions, improved manufacturing and supply chain flexibility, improved product quality, and improved customer service.

Of course, it's not feasible to turn every employee into a Kaizen black belt. But it is possible to smooth out the change process. All it takes is a little motivation.

Chapter 47: Conclusion

Lean is how a properly designed and operated supply chain should function. A Lean Supply Chain process is one that has been streamlined to reduce and eliminate waste or non-value added activities along the supply chain flow associated with the movement of products.

Waste can be measured in time, inventory and unnecessary costs. Value-added activities are those that contribute to efficiently placing the final product at the customer's door.

The supply chain and inventory contained in the chain should flow. Any activity that stops the flow or that touches inventory should create value.

Lean supply chain management is not just for manufacturers who practice lean manufacturing. Nor is it just for large retailers. It is a practice that can benefit small and mid-size home furnishings retailers, wholesalers, distributors and others.

Supply chains tend to accrue waste and non-value added activities for many reasons, both internal to the company and external. Regaining lean supply chain efficiencies may mean addressing many of the same issues that created the problems of extra and unneeded time, inventory and costs.

The ideal approach is to design the perfect supply chain and fit your company's operation onto it.

Supply chain management is meant to reduce excess inventory in the supply chain. It should be demand driven, built on the "pull" approach of customers pulling inventory in a flow as required, not by suppliers pushing inventory. Excess inventory reflects the additional time spent within the supply chain operation. So the perfect supply chain is lean, having removed wasteful time and inventory.

A lean supply chain, with the pull, flows back from the store floor through to purchase orders placed on suppliers. Anything that delays or impedes this flow must be analyzed as a potential non-value added activity.

What must be done to be Lean

1. Understand that this is an ongoing, continuous improvement approach as compared to business process reengineering which can be viewed as a one-time change.
2. Gain top management's commitment. Continuous improvement requires ongoing support.
3. Build a multi-discipline team for the project; one that understands lean supply chain management.
4. Analyze the total supply chain process, not just the outbound or just the inbound part.
5. Map the process.
6. Assess for gaps or redundancies in the process that create time, the key waste.

7. Avoid cannibalizing the process by just focusing on warehousing or transportation or other activities instead of studying the entire supply chain process.

8. Realize cause-effect impacts. High freight cost, for example, can be a problem or a symptom.

9. Excess inventory can be a problem or, more often, a symptom of a problem.

10. Drive for root causes, not symptoms.

11. Comprehend the complexity of supply chains with multiple suppliers, distribution centres and stores.

12. Appreciate the fundamental impact of international sourcing and shipping on time and inventory.

13. Grasp the impact of the organization and culture on supply chain process design and operation. This can be overlooked as a factor in achieving or not achieving lean.

14. Analyze the effect of continuing external events, such as Homeland Security activities or imports, on lead times and on lean dynamics.

15. Calculate the risks of the lean supply chain. Reducing inventory frees up capital; reducing time improves the cash-to-cash cycle. However reducing inventory, without a properly designed process, removes the comfortable feeling that accompanies excess inventory and can expose you to the risk of lost sales.

16. Observe the effect that time has on inventory and on an effective process.
17. Assess where standardization is feasible and where customizing to specific customer requirements is needed.
18. Demand supplier performance. It is vital to a lean supply chain operation.
19. Measure the present process as total cycle time, costs and inventory (both in dollars and units) and inventory turns.
20. Integrate the supply chain. Breaks in the flow, both internal and external, can be pockets of waste.
21. Identify non-value added activities, their effect and their cause.
22. Rationalize the process.
23. Improve the process to drive change.
24. Streamline the process for unnecessary complexity as well as unnecessary suppliers and service providers.
25. Incorporate technology, such as supply chain execution technology, as part of the process improvement.

Good Luck!

Resource and References

Shigeo Shingo, Norman Bodek, Collin McLoughlin: Kaizen and the Art of Creative Thinking - The Scientific Thinking Mechanism

Shigeo Shingo; Fundamental Principles of Lean Manufacturing

Shigeo Shingo, Andrew P. Dillon (Translator); Zero Quality Control: Source Inspection and the Poka-yoke System

Shigeo Shingo; Non-Stock Production: The Shingo System of Continuous Improvement

Shigeo Shingo; A Study of the Toyota Production System from an Industrial Engineering Viewpoint

Shigeo Shingo; A Study of the Toyota Production System from an Industrial Engineering Viewpoint

Drucker, P. (1993) Post-Capitalist Society

Drucker, P., "What Makes an Effective Executive", Harvard Business review, June 2004

Lessons from Toyota's long drive, an interview with Katsuaki Watanabe, HBR, July 2007

Liker, J. & D. Meier, Toyota Talent, McGraw Hill, 2007

Shook, J. , Managing To Learn, Lean Enterprise Institute 2008

Fishman, C., "No Satisfaction", Fast Company, Dec 2006/Jan 2007

Womack, J. & J. Shook, Lean Management and The Role of Lean Leadership, Lean Enterprise Institute presentation, Oct. 2006